'Society has earned a rest from your acti...'

C000261367

TWIN... OR 30 YEARS

The luxurious main ball

The 10 men sent to jail today

The Kray case sentences at the Old Bailey today were:

RONALD KRAY, aged 35, of Bunhill Row, Clerkenwell: life imprisonment, that he be detained for 30 years.

REGINALD KRAY, aged 35, also of Bunhill Row, Clerkenwell: life, 30 years recommended, and on second charge, 10 years to run concurrently.

JOHN BARRIE, aged 51 of no fixed address: life, 20 years recommended.

RONALD BENDER aged 30, of Gabriel Gardens, Poplar: life, 20 years recommended.

ANTHONY LAMBRIANOU, aged 26, of Blythe Road Bethnal Green: life, 15 years recommended.

CHRISTOPHER LAMBRIANOU, aged 29, of Queensbridge Road Hackney: life, 15 years recommended.

CHARLES KRAY, 41, of Rosefield Gardens Tower Hamlets: 10 years.

FREDERICK FORMAN, aged 36, of ... Street, Southwark: ... years.

CORNELIUS WHITEHEAD, aged 28, of ... Gardens, ... Hamlets: seven years.

ALBERT DONAGHUE aged 33, of Devons ... Bow: two years.

By STUART FRIEND, CYRIL LING and MICHAEL McDONOUGH

The Kray twins, Ronald and Reginald, aged 35, were sentenced at the Old Bailey today for murder.

Mr Justice Melford Stevenson said: 'I am not going to waste words on you. I sentence you to life imprisonment. In my view society has earned a rest from your activities and I recommend you to be detained for 30 years.'

The sentences on the Krays are the longest for murder ever handed at the Old Bailey.

John Barrie

And brother Charles gets ten years

Charles Kray, 41-year-old brother of the twins, was one of the eight others sentenced by Mr Justice Melford Stevenson at the Old Bailey today.

The judge said the maximum sentence he could pass for his crime of being an accessory after the murder of McVitie was ten years.

Axeman case

Bouquet of tulips from the jury

MILITARY TRAGEDY IN LONDON.

MAJOR MILES CHARLES SETON, R.C. ITALIAN MEDICAL CORPS THE VICTIM OF THE TRAGEDY

SIR MALCOLM SETON, AN ADMIRALTY OFFICIAL, WHOSE BROTHER HE ...

ANNIE CHAPMAN BEFORE AND AFTER DEATH

'THE DE... THE PUBLIC OWES'

During the sentences the judge praised police who were involved in the investigations.

A WHITECHAPEL SLAUGHTER YARD.

OR PAGES SIX AND SEVEN

Kray's Empire muscle and mur...

Tragedy of th... beautiful brid...

Kings gone—n... battle for cro...

HATRY SENTENCED TO 14 YE...

FALL GUILTY, JURY ASKS MERCY

scape

$1,000,000 Wiped Out Here in Day

EX-SECRETARY CONVICTED FOR BRIBERY DEAL

DOWNFALL OF WALL STREET HITS WICHITA

Brokerage Offices Here Swamped by Customers

PRAISES CITY

STOCK MARKET STRUGGLES TO REMAIN STEADY

Broad Advance at Opening Held With Difficulty as Sales Mount

DIES

MAN WITH CUT THROAT ALONE FOR TWO DAYS

Would-Be Suicide Is Found Slowly Bleeding to Death

GUILTY!

Dramatic Scene in Court as Doheny Denounces Trial Judge

MRS. COOLIDGE'S MOTHER IS DEAD

Mrs. Lemira Goodhue Succumbs After Illness of Two Years

The Illustrated
Story of CRIME

The Illustrate
Story o

CRIME

Edgar Lustgarten

Weidenfeld and Nicolson London

Previous pages, left to right: (top) Ronald True, Horatio
Bottomley, Bruno Richard Hauptmann; (bottom)
Leopold and Loeb, Gaston Dominici, Rasputin,
Mussolini.

ISBN 0 297 77196 5

Designed by John Rushton Associates
for George Weidenfeld and Nicolson Ltd.,
11 St John's Hill, London SW11

Filmset by Keyspools Limited, Golborne, Lancs.
Printed in Great Britain by
Morrison & Gibb Limited, Edinburgh.

for Donald

Qui s'excuse *page 9*

Contents

Previous pages: left, Assassination of Spencer
Perceval; right, A Jack the Ripper Suspect.

Qui s'excuse

If I were not interested in crime, I would not be writing this book. If you were not interested in crime, you would not be reading it. But why *should* we be interested – either you or I? In my case, to such an extent that writing and reading about crime has occupied a large proportion of my adult life.

Bearing the contemptuous tag of 'crime aficionados', we are commonly charged with depravity of taste, morbidity of mind, a preference for what is bad rather than what is good. Unfounded charges, except against a negligible minority. Most of us can honestly plead Not Guilty to all counts; most of us in fairness are entitled to acquittal. We are drawn towards the study of crime as towards any other window which opens on human nature – and not many such windows offer so clear a view. That view is by no means uniformly beautiful, but the window cannot be held responsible for the prospect. 'Wherever you find human nature,' as Dr Johnson said, 'there is a mixture of vice and virtue, a contest of passions and reason.' Crime is composed mostly of the vices and the passions; seldom mixed with reason, with virtue hardly ever. Nevertheless it forms a massive part of human nature, and can no more be ignored in a review of our own species than can disease, injury, war, pestilence or death. That is why crime has fascinated writers as diverse as Tennyson Jesse and De Quincey, Dostoevsky and Poe.

There are, of course, two schools of writing about crime. The main aim of one is to probe psychology – and thereby to illuminate and instruct. The main aim of the other is to tell a story – and thereby to divert and entertain. The same writer, though, at the same time, may attach to both schools. Like those already named; like Zola (*Thérèse Raquin*), Emlyn Williams (*Beyond Belief*), Truman Capote (*In Cold Blood*), Graham Greene (*Brighton Rock*). In that breakdown of categories, where do *I* belong?

It is for the reader, not for me, eventually to say. I can only make here a Declaration of Intent. It is notoriously harder to prove a negative than a positive; let me then first try to expound that aspect. This book is not meant to be a history of crime – exhaustive, comprehensive, even chronological. It is not meant to be a scientific (or pseudo-scientific) exercise. It is not meant to be a medical (or medico-legal) treatise. Above all, it is not meant to be a 'criminological' conceit, theorizing on causality and penology. I claim no greater knowledge about any facet of crime than that obtainable from normal reading and experience, plus what may have been garnered over a span of years spent as a practising advocate in the criminal courts.

Very well. It may justifiably be asked: On that foundation, from those sources, what are you now setting out to do?

I invite any inquirer to consider the headings in the table of contents. They constitute the blueprint, the ground plan, for the work. They are the major themes which I have extracted from the never-ending devil's symphony of crime. Taken together, with illustrations – verbal and pictorial – they should provide a broad conspectus of the criminal scene. If that illuminates and instructs, all to the good. If it also entertains and diverts, so much the better.

To provide that conspectus is my task, as I regard it. Lessons I leave to be inferred by the beholder. Thus early, at any rate, only one would I suggest – one that I myself learn afresh each day I live. Crime is fundamentally unchanging – and unchanged. Most of the individual cases which will be examined are relatively recent – within the last ten, fifty or a hundred years. But make no mistake; that is not to mark any general historical shift. They vary only superficially from predecessors. Social changes may bring in their wake new opportunities. Technological changes may bring in their wake new methods. Changes in moral ethos may bring in their wake new sanctions, which sometimes encourage new offences (and new defences, too). But crime, in its essence, is immutable as mankind, of which it is such a primary and awful manifestation. No measures to oppose it can be more than containing measures; no remedies can be more than palliatives. A decline in crime is never other than temporary. Nor can the number of its basic varieties be reduced. Cut off one of the heads of crime as often as you may, and, like one of the hydra's, it will sprout again and flourish. I do not trade in 'messages' but if I did, that would be mine.

It will be noted that no chapter is allocated to murders, other than those of a political character. But murder constantly crops up in the course of, and commission of, other crimes, such as rape, kidnapping, Gang activities; sometimes wilfully (in exuberance of evil), sometimes compulsively (for instance, elimination of witnesses). It seemed better to treat each case in its particular context, rather than assemble all into a separate group. I estimate that murders will easily outnumber any other crime considered in the following pages. Certainly the arrangement adopted does not signify any departure by the author from the received opinion that murder is the wickedest and gravest of all crimes.

1.

GANGS AND GANGSTERS

Al Capone
Frank Costello
Joe Adonis
the Messinas
the Krays
the Mafia

There is a world of difference between a Gang (spelt with a large G) and a 'gang' (spelt with a small one). The etymological resemblance serves only to mislead.

Consider first the 'gang'. A group of wrongdoers who combine in wrongdoing. But, in their case, against whom? Individual citizens. By what means? Theft, cheating, or assault. To what end? Direct gain or personal satisfaction. Examples of the 'gang', in every age and land, are many: the Indian Thugs; the Neapolitan Camorra; Robin Hood's men, who attacked the rich in eleventh-century England; the Chauffeurs, who plundered lonely farms in eighteenth-century France; the Kellys, who rustled cattle in nineteenth-century Australia. Each recognizably, unmistakably, a 'gang'. Their similarities leap the frontiers of space and time. The 'gang' has no special period, no special provenance.

Consider now the Gang. Also a group of wrongdoers who combine in wrongdoing. But, in their case, against whom?

PAGE 12: Ned Kelly photographed shortly before his execution

RIGHT: The body of Joe Byrne, a leading member of the Kelly gang who was killed in an ambush, strung up outside Benalla police station to be photographed

Established authority. By what means? Illegal force or subornation. To what end? Spheres of influence, territory, control. Examples of the Gang, until recent years and then within restricted zones, are nil; yet another point where it diverges from the 'gang', and still the list of contrasts is far from being complete. Unlike the 'gangs', the Gangs seldom wage war against the public. Unlike the 'gangs', they frequently wage war between themselves. Rival 'gangs' will not fight over a pocket to be picked or a pigeon to be plucked. But when rival Gangs claim fief over a 'manor', they will almost always clash and sometimes blood is spilt. A 'gang', if it kills, commonly kills an innocent victim. A Gangster, if he kills, commonly kills a Gangster. One of them took a virtuous pride in this distinction. 'What the hell,' he said. 'We only kill each other.'

Above all, while the scope of 'gangs' is boundless, that of Gangs can be defined with relative precision. Historically and

geographically. The Gang *has* a special period, a special provenance. It is a phenomenon of the twentieth century. It originated in the United States.

The remote genesis of Gangs was the Great Migration westwards. Dwarfing the earlier movement (from northern Europe and from Ireland), this second stream assumed the magnitude of a torrent, of a flood. The immigrants now were mostly from southern and eastern Europe, although Ireland still contributed a sizeable share. They fled from poverty, persecution, revolutions, wars – the Old World's old maladies, old torments, old afflictions. Their ancestors had endured; they had had no option. The advent of the steamship opened up the seas.

Thousands made for England. It was the shortest, cheapest, journey. But hundreds of thousands contrived the transatlantic passage. Rumours, newspapers, letters home from pioneers, told of American plenty – and American potential. Food, jobs, high wages, vast expansion. All that and toleration, too. Truly the Land of Promise. Truly the gift of God.

BELOW: Lucky Luciano, one of the most notorious Mafia bosses. He was eventually deported from the United States after serving a ten-year prison sentence

On the loaded boats, though, responding to the magnet, bad elements mingled with the good. When the Promise – or the fantasy – fell short of fulfilment, the reaction of those bad elements ran true to form. What they could not get from God, they tried to get from crime. Especially the Irish. Especially the Italians. As they introduced the best, they introduced the worst. The country that gave America Fiorello La Guardia also gave America Lucky Luciano. The country that gave America John F. Kennedy also gave America Dion O'Banion. The Lucianos and the O'Banions were not, as a rule, an immediate product of the Great Migration. The scum actually cast ashore with the main influx was absorbed initially by the scum already there. Unimportant and obscure in their devious traffics, neither they nor their offshoots would ever have been otherwise but for the blind aiding and abetting of their hosts. The gates to infinite illicit gold were opened wide by the Eighteenth Amendment to the Constitution, which, in 1920, made America 'dry'. That Amendment was the proximate genesis of Gangs.

Today most Americans are completely at a loss to understand how Prohibition ever happened. The explanation is

simple. It was popular. When Congress passed the Volstead Act (which gave the Amendment teeth), national sentiment overwhelmingly approved. There seems to have been a vision of communal redemption through universal abstinence from alcohol.

ABOVE: Watched by Lucky and friends, a priest blesses a new Luciano business venture

If so, the vision faded. Dramatically and fast. Prohibition, instead of exorcizing drink, transformed it from an indulgence into a necessity. Drys became wets; wets wetter; Chicago (which, against the trend, had voted heavily wet) became, by every indication, wettest spot of all. The bootleggers – almost without exception immigrants who found themselves up to the eyes in dollars overnight – noted those indications and planned accordingly. The effect was to inflict on America's second largest city 'such an epidemic of killings' – I quote F. L. Allen's *Only Yesterday* – 'as no civilized modern city had ever before seen.'

That epidemic, while it lasted, raged like a forest fire. It established Chicago as the prototypal Gang town. It provided the setting for the prototypal Gangster.

Alphonse ('Al') Capone, fourth son of Gabriel and Teresa, was born in Brooklyn in 1899. His parents were decent folk, apparently fated to be poor. Six years earlier they had sold their little grocer's shop and sailed from their native Italy in quest of better fortune. The quest was not successful. They understood no English, had no particular skills, and, as humble shopkeepers without patronage or connections, found New York as unremunerative as Naples. They remained, however, what they had always been: honest, patient, hard-working, law-abiding. Their fourth son did not derive his character from them. Mendelians may speculate upon his forbears; myself I believe such speculations profitless. The main responsibility for being what he was rests upon his own broad and hefty shoulders.

His environment, of course, should not be totally ignored. It did provide temptations – and opportunities. Capone's home ground was an overcrowded slum speckled with sleazy clubs, swarming with cutprice whores, a nursery of adolescent 'gangs' which roamed the streets. Being pugnacious, unafraid, effective with his outsized fists (and soon with deadlier weapons), he quickly matured from juvenile rowdy into hardened rough. Still in his teens, he was a bouncer at a brothel. Still in his teens, he was barman at a rendezvous for crooks. Still in his teens, he was severely slashed during a knife fight – slashes that left facial scars later as widely known as Von Stroheim's scalp or as Durante's nose. He was thus apprenticed (of his own accord) to crime; he was presently committed (of his own accord) to crime; but nothing suggested a limelit future as a master criminal. Everything suggested merely a dim succession of equivalent episodes, a dangerous and squalid life which was not even lucrative, an end – early rather than late – passing quite unnoticed except on a few corners between Broadway and the Bowery. It would probably have happened that way, but for Johnny Torrio.

Capone's odious immortality, the very fact that I am impelled to write and you to read about him, depended on a whole series of contingencies relating to himself and Johnny Torrio. If Torrio had not been a flourishing local hoodlum. If one of his dens had not been close to the Capones' dark tenement. If the half-grown bandit had not caught Torrio's eye. If Torrio had not used him to lead young accomplices (an inverted form of Sherlock Holmes's Baker Street irregulars). If Capone had not shown himself eager, self-reliant. If Torrio had not deserted New York for Chicago to serve his uncle, Big Jim Colosimo, as an aide. If Torrio had not, in due course, summoned from New York a gratified Capone to serve as aide to *him*. If, in 1920, Big Jim had not been murdered. If Torrio had not succeeded as leader of his Gang. If, in 1925, an attempt had not been made to murder Torrio, who consequently lost his nerve and prudently 'retired'. If Capone had not by then been more a partner than an aide. Subtract one link from that chain and you preclude the crucial moment – the moment when Capone succeeded Torrio, and embarked upon a ruthless, bloody, reign of power which has no parallel in Gangster history. Almost incredibly Capone was barely twenty-six when it began and had not reached thirty-two when it was all over. Quite a short run really, though it didn't seem so. At least not in Chicago. At least not at the time.

Chicago was never a model of propriety. It was a vice town long before it was a Gang town; the Levee competed nationally with New York's Tenderloin. Certain Chicago 'gangs' had long been in existence; some (such as the white slavers) linked with the Levee, some quite unconnected (such as the Black Hand – felonious immigrants who extorted 'tribute' from more worthy immigrants who had prospered and made good). Later, but still well ahead of the First World War, what are identifiable as real Gangs took shape; they added their own turbulence to a turbulent community, but by stealth, anonymously, out of public view. In the days of Big Jim's predominance, for instance, there were no disorders singling out Chicago from a dozen other cities in the USA. Ordinary people elsewhere had never heard of him, nor did their pulses quicken at the mention of his base. The centre of Illinois was not yet a byword. Chicago's fame – Chicago's shame – waited on Capone.

It has been claimed that Capone was an innovator. That claim can only be sustained in the narrowest sense. He was not a creative criminal like Bottomley or Haigh, inventing fresh methods, devising fresh techniques. But if he lacked capacity for forming new ideas, he possessed great capacity for improving upon old ones. Anything you can do I can do better. Better usually. Invariably *bigger*.

One example: determining the range of Gang activities –
whether productive or 'supervisory'.

Big Jim's major trade had been in women (both for the
home consumer and for export). Torrio got it organized
efficiently. Big Jim's minor trade had been in gaming (both at
a smart night joint and in shabbier rooms). Torrio got it
organized efficiently. Big Jim only lived to see the dawn of
Prohibition, but had given prompt priority to bootlegging.
Torrio got it organized efficiently. Torrio's accession to top
place coincided with easy urban access to the countryside by
car; roving spenders meant a boom in road houses, and
Torrio added several to the Gang's fixed assets. It accorded
with his policy (successfully pressed on Uncle) of having
fingers in different pies, eggs in different baskets – diversify-
ing, as they say in company reports. Doubtless Torrio would
discuss this policy with his aide. Doubtless his aide would
manifest agreement.

In all sincerity. Capone did agree upon the policy. He only
disagreed upon its application. Torrio's purview never went
beyond a segment of Gang fodder either in the heart or the
suburbs of Chicago. The older man tempered enterprise with
caution; on guard continually lest he overreached. As long as
Torrio remained, Capone followed suit; but, on assuming
full control, he made the sky the limit. Diversification need
not stop at booze and road houses; should not stick at
outposts in Blue Island or Burnham. He took in horse and dog
tracks, waterway and truck fleets, industrial associations,
labour unions; reached out to the coasts, the Canadian
frontier, wherever booty beckoned and Thompson shooters
spoke. Even more than a despot's growing megalomania,
what drew him on was the lure of funds essential to support a
life-style suddenly turned lavish to the point of lunacy. His
bespoke, armour-plated, Cadillac sedan, outriders fore and
aft – all right, a business expense. His GHQ, two whole floors
of a luxury hotel – all right, with a Gang a thousand strong, a
business expense. His huge subventions to his mother,
brothers, sisters – all right, family fondness, not vulgar
ostentation. His bounty to the poor, in money and in kind – all
right, generous sympathy, not morbid superstition. But the
diamond necklaces he gave his mistresses, the diamond belts
he gave his pals, the diamond rings he wore – these were the

excesses of an exhibitionist. They vastly increased already vast expenditure, but he neither ran down capital nor ran up debts. At peak, his gross revenue – I don't mean before paying tax, Capone *didn't* pay it – was not measured in hundreds of thousands (like Big Jim's at *his* peak), nor in millions (like Torrio's at *his*), but in hundreds of millions of dollars every year.

A second example of Capone's going one better and one bigger: the extent of his dominion over 'the Authorities'.

There was nothing novel about Gangsters doing business with enforcement officers and proxies of the law. Big Jim had done it, Torrio had done it, their competitors had done it or had tried to. A 'subscription' to a grafting alderman. A 'present' to a senior clerk in the DA's office. A wad of greenbacks – tattered and untraceable – to cops. In tacit exchange for municipal 'concessions'. For turning a blind eye. For making themselves scarce. 'Grease' was always an item in the Gangster's kit. He bought, as well as sold, 'protection'.

Again, Capone did not depart from tested policy. Again, though, he enlarged enormously its range. He bypassed cops, clerks, even aldermen. He collected police chiefs, governors, even judges. He did not merely bribe them. He hired them. He owned them. They were on his pay roll. They carried out his orders – if they didn't, woe betide. When one suburban mayor had incurred his displeasure, Capone knocked him down the town hall steps and kicked him as he lay. A patrolman, seeing it happen, discreetly moved along. Capone demanded absolute obedience from his puppets. Besides, he stored liquor in the vaults of that town hall.

Admittedly, he went to work on bent material. Undeniably, he bent it to the last extreme. It was expensive, but his investment paid off a hundredfold. He made his person sacrosanct, his henchmen nearly so. Crimes there were galore; brutal, vicious, crimes; known to all as the crimes of Capone and his Gang. And yet arrests were few, prosecutions were still fewer, convictions fewer still, the minute residue of sentences nominal or nullified. The blameless president of Chicago's impotent crime commission later tersely summarized the situation. 'Al Capone ran the city,' he lamented.

A third example of Capone sharpening old procedures rather than promoting new: his idiosyncratic use of violence.

Already Gangs and violence appeared inseparable. Violence was the Gangster's sign manual, his trade mark. Capone entered a Chicago where the Gangs equalled in violence – as they surpassed in size – their counterparts elsewhere. But the customary Gang weapon was a blackjack, the customary Gang practice was a beating up. A gun was a rarity, a murder an exception. Appropriately, Gang commandos were styled 'muscle men'.

Capone did not dispense with unarmed muscle men. They were adequate for dealing with daily chores – frightening traders, chasing 'debts', hauling contraband. But many of his swelling army – certainly his bodyguards – secreted their ultimate argument in a holster, slung across the left shoulder underneath the jacket. And also – Capone's most original conception – he simultaneously mechanized and camouflaged his spearheads by putting marksmen with tommy guns in autos without licence plates. Against such outfits, Gangs relying on old-fashioned equipment stood about as much chance in a head-on collision as the Polish cavalry against the German Panzers. They imitated and they emulated – but too late. Capone, having won the lead, kept a jump ahead. No one could wrest from him his overall supremacy. The desperate efforts made had only one effect: to step up Gang warfare to unprecedented heights of hatred and recklessness and audacity. The headline years began; the years when daylight battles flared in busy streets; the years when typists and tycoons ran frantically for cover while Gangsters, from car or roof or window, shot it out.

Inevitably, many died from Gangster bullets (including a few for whom they were not meant). Yet, although he caused hundreds of those deaths, it would not be right to say that Capone was trigger happy. He never murdered merely for the sake of murder; he would have considered that un-businesslike and wasteful. But he coldly executed anyone who crossed him, who didn't play ball, who wouldn't get out of his way. And if there was also an ingredient of vengeance, of returning blow for blow, of paying off a score, then Capone's malevolence bordered on satanic. As in the best remembered of his infamies, the St Valentine's Day Massacre of 1929.

By then, among what opposition to Capone survived, Bugs Moran was the only serious contender. Moran's challenges were not to be despised, and one or two tactical successes boosted his assurance. He hi-jacked Capone's trucks, bombed Capone's saloons, came near to rubbing out Capone's ace triggerman. Each, to some degree, injured Capone's business; each, to a much greater degree, injured Capone's pride. He took them as insults, as personal affronts, to be requited only by most sanguinary measures. So he devised a fiendish plot, set the wheels revolving, briefed a picked squad of his experienced lieutenants, and – several weeks before the date assigned for action – went to his house in Florida, a thousand miles away.

BELOW: Capone's luxurious Florida retreat where he carefully staged his alibi for the Valentine's Massacre

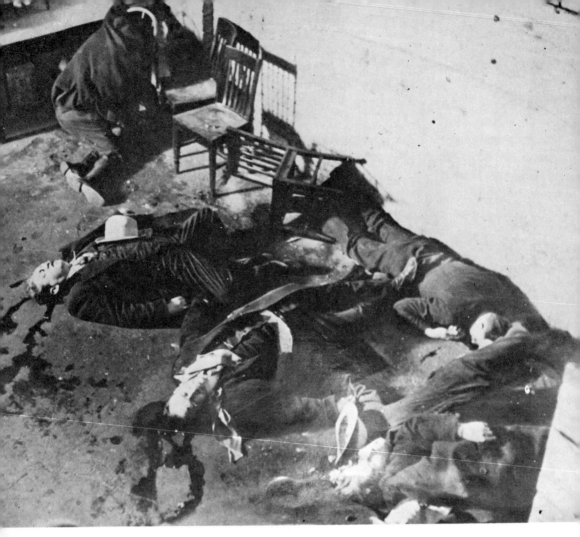

ABOVE: The St
Valentine's Day
Massacre, 1929

On 13 February, a trusted supplier phoned Moran to offer
him a load of whisky at a bargain price. Moran told him to
deliver it at half past ten next morning. Moran was late for the
appointment, and thereby saved his life; seven of his Gang,
though, were waiting in his warehouse. Unexpectedly arrived
what seemed to be a police car, with regulation gadgets and
regulation gong; two men in uniform, three men in plain
clothes. Moran's Gang, who were heavily armed, would have
fought Capone's like tigers; but, altogether hoodwinked,
thought resistance ill-advised. As Capone had foreseen, they
allowed the uniformed raiders to disarm them; whereupon
the plain clothes men, pointing tommy guns, advanced and
lined them up against the wall. Three times they swung the
guns – at stomach, chest and head. Then they vanished,
leaving behind a morgue.

24

No one was ever brought to book for this atrocity, although the guiding hand was recognized by half the world. Capone, however, had a cast-iron alibi. At the very moment when the seven bodies slumped like riddled sacks to the floor of Moran's warehouse, he was at the county solicitor's office in Miami, talking about his future projects as a resident.

The St Valentine's Day Massacre marked the climacteric of Capone's career – and, indeed, of the type of Gangsterdom he stood for. After that, he moved in only one direction. Down.

Three months later, he received a prison term: a year – the maximum – for carrying a gun. True, it was in Philadelphia, beyond his sovereignty; he may even have invited temporary shelter from Moran. Nonetheless, his humiliation must have been acute. While he was in jail, the Great Bull Market crashed; he came out into the shadows of the Great Depression, where even super-Gang chiefs found the living not so easy. Chicago's administration had been purged and cleansed; the new men actually clamped down on Capone. Finally, the Internal Revenue moved in. The Gangster who had made the law a laughing-stock, who had flouted governments, who time and again had literally got away with murder, was at long last despatched to Alcatraz – for what? Failing to pay his income tax.

BELOW: Capone and his attorney at the Federal Grand Jury hearing. Capone was charged with tax evasion

The arch-criminal proved a model prisoner. His long sentence accordingly curtailed, he was released in 1939. Sick, broken, confronted with a different world, he never attempted to resume his life of crime. In 1947 he died of a brain haemorrhage during the tertiary stage of neurosyphilis. He had contracted the disease almost twenty years before from an inmate of a whorehouse he controlled.

The Chicago of Capone has left an indelible stain on the American twenties. Perpetuated in plays, films, novels. And no wonder. No other Gangsters, no other Gangs, ever afforded artists such raw material. So bizarre that it had to be understated and played down. 'Scarface' and 'On the Spot' did not go further than Capone. Capone went further than 'On the Spot' and 'Scarface'.

The departure of Capone from the Gangland scene was shortly followed by the repeal of Prohibition. The one event heralded, the other sealed, the end of the first era of the Gangs. The second era, which began with hardly any pause between, may have been no less vicious. It was certainly less lurid. That was due in part to choice, in part to circumstances.

Bootlegging had vanished on the instant, overnight. What could be substituted as the Gangster's primary livelihood? They would hold no formal conference, but all the same they had to reappraise their strategy. No new rackets lay open to development; only some which, during Prohibition, had been sidelines. The problem was to pick the one most promising and suitable for fuller exploitation. Murder 'contracts'? Minimum turnover, maximum risk. Narcotics? A growth industry, but a pigmy beside booze. Girls? Commerce inconveniently restricted by the Mann Act (which rendered you liable to heavy punishment if you transported a woman across State lines for immoral purposes). These, it was decided, were best retained as sidelines, while the Gangs concentrated on illegal gambling; at all levels, and in every form. Compared to bootlegging, the gambling racket did not tend to touch off nearly so much violence – a fact that harmonized with the prevailing Gangster mood.

For reaction was strong against Capone-type operations. His successors felt he had given Gangsters a bad name. They tried to erase this unfortunate impression by concluding agreements and peacefully picketing, instead of coercing brutally and provoking wars. They did not renounce violence, but used it sparingly. They did not rule out murder, but held it back as the last card. There were to be no more flying bullets, no more fleeing passers-by, no replicas, no repetitions of St Valentine. To borrow a favourite phrase from latter-day journalese, the Gangsters aimed henceforth at keeping a low profile. Accordingly they altered their social image and attire. Capone – always, of course, heavily escorted – had flaunted himself like a superstar at the opera and at ball games; had worn flamboyant suits of lilac, orange and magenta; had sported boaters with gaudy bands, or curly-brimmed fedoras. Had done everything, in fact, to draw public attention. On the other hand, the *nouvelle vague* wooed personal obscurity; dressed conservatively in sober hues; eschewed irrelevant

ABOVE: Shielding her face from photographers, Mae Capone visits her husband in Alcatraz

27

adornments. Did everything, in fact, to escape public attention. They looked, and tried their best to sound, like business executives, which – if only as a cover – many of them were. They moved, says Alistair Cooke in his book *America*, 'with masterly discretion into real estate, banking, the export–import trade in drugs, the control of supermarkets, hotels, big and little corporations, so that today nobody is sure where legitimate business ends and the syndicate [that is, the Gang conglomerates] takes over.' But, beneath the smooth exterior, their interests were unchanged. They were 'white-collar Capones', Estes Kefauver wrote.

Kefauver had better opportunities than most of assessing them from observation at close quarters. He was chairman of the Senate Crime Investigating Committee (far better known simply by his name) which held public sittings all over the Union between May 1950 and May 1951. From these sittings it transpired that there were two major Gangs – each with infinite ramifications – in the United States. One, based on Chicago, was composed of Capone leftovers who had adapted to contemporary requirements. The other, based on New York, wielded greater power; its boss, Frank Costello, and its sub-boss, Joe Adonis, expediently obeyed Kefauver summonses.

Costello (real name, Francesco Castiglia), called by insiders the Prime Minister of Crime, was the most influential

BELOW: Frank Costello before the Senate Crime Investigating Committee

figure in the American underworld. Sixty years old, impeccably groomed, conspicuously manicured, he protested that the Committee's charges against him were unfounded and, with pained dignity, requested their retraction. But, after seven days of incisive questioning, he confessed to so many of them that he left the stand whimpering, whining, mopping an anguished brow.

Adonis (real name Joseph Doto) cut a better figure. Or a worse – it depends on your criteria. He never whimpered, never whined, never mopped an anguished brow. On the contrary, he was downright contemptuous. He also, though, affected ripe respectability, a pose more easily sustained with his well-cut, iron-grey hair. But Kefauver considered him even more sinister than Costello – 'the personification of modern criminality'.

Both Costello and Adonis were men of the sort you would expect to see lunching at the Waldorf. Both were men of the sort that you *would* see lunching at the Waldorf. Unostentatious. Undistinguishable from other customers. Typical Gangsters of the second and third era. Not national talking points like Capone had been. Not subjects for plays, novels, films like Capone had been. They sought neither his spurious glamour nor his sticky end. Long before the Senate Crime Committee, soon after Capone's downfall, that part of his legacy had been transferred to England.

It began with the Messinas. The one Gang of which I can write with firsthand knowledge. The one Gang I ever actually saw at work.

Those Mediterranean dregs – the family had been flung out of Sicily, Malta, Egypt, Morocco, Spain – descended on London in 1932, when a semblance of peace had just descended on Chicago. Previously, England had only rudimentary Gangs; most, like those portrayed by Graham Greene in *Brighton Rock*, confining themselves to the racecourse fringe and its subsidiaries. On the majority of people they made no real impact. Nor, for quite a number of years, did the Messinas. The police must have been acutely conscious of their presence. Occasionally they cropped up in Parliament or Press – in questions or articles implying they were a vice ring. But the name, if ever noted, quickly was forgotten. The man in the street – unlike the woman on the streets – knew as little about them as some ministers seemed to know. Ordinary eyes detected no material change in the undisguised machine of prostitution. Mine certainly did not – until, in 1947, I moved into the Albany.

The Albany ('quaint, old-fashioned', say the guide books) is a private enclave off Piccadilly, with a back entrance (traditionalists call it the North Gate) on Burlington Gardens, facing Savile Row. The nearest pub to that entrance was *The Sunderland* (since bulldozed to accommodate an office block), which I took to dropping in at most evenings for a pint. It was frequented (although not for picking up) by a lot of the girls who plied on Regent Street; as fellow regulars, we would exchange small talk. One night, arriving later than usual, almost at closing time, I told Big Gwennie (so addressed by all the others) of a strange occurrence I had witnessed on my way. A woman I had often seen before at the same spot was standing, obviously hoping for a client. A white Rolls-Royce drew up. A swarthy man got out. There was the briefest conversation in the lowest tones. Then the man, moving closer to her, flashed a razor. The woman screamed and ran for dear life. In flight she dropped her handbag, did not stop to pick it up, never slackened speed till she reached the strollers along Bond Street, where she vanished round the corner without once looking back. '*Very* odd,' I said, in my innocence. 'Not odd at all,' Big Gwennie said, fear clouding her plump face. 'I can tell you who that geezer was. One of the Messinas.'

RIGHT: Eugene and Carmelo Messina

With an effort, I recalled the name's significance. From then on, I systematically took cognisance of what was happening after dark outside my very door. As a result, three years later, when the whole story broke, I felt like one who has already seen the pictures and can now read the book.

A phrase may be beautiful or ugly to the *ear*; that depends entirely on its *sound*. A phrase may be beautiful or ugly to the *mind*; that depends entirely on its *associations*. These sometimes are added to, subtracted from, supplanted. None has suffered more in this respect than 'Band of Brothers'. Once it recalled the few – the happy few – that fought upon Saint Crispin's Day. Now it is as likely to recall the vile few that smeared the Mayfair pavements upon innumerable nights.

There were five of them. Salvatore, Alfredo, Eugene, Carmelo, Attilio. The same five, in the same order, that of age – Mr Evans, Mr Martin, Mr Marshall, Mr Maitland, Mr Maynard. They used these aliases when acquiring houses. It drew less suspicion. They used their own surname professionally. It struck more dread.

Poncing is not a new profession. It is the second oldest. And the Messinas *were* ponces; they took money earned by prostitutes they lived with. But they greatly extended the idea. Not only did they tax the sale of sex by wife or consort; they taxed a host of other prostitutes as well. So many that the brothers grew extremely rich; able to buy costly homes and cars and clothes – and also any human being, female or male, who was in the market to be bought.

The Messina prostitutes resembled foreign mercenaries. With rare exceptions, they were imports from abroad. Predominantly French – for at least one good reason. Mam'selle's accent, Mam'selle's coquetry ('Allo darling, looking for a naughtee girl?'), traditionally awake desire among sluggish Englishmen. The Messina recruitment of Mam'selles had a uniform pattern; applied alike to Picardy peasants dazzled by dreams of Angleterre, and to Pigalle veterans who had been warned to scram. First came the pledges: smart address, expensive garb, domestic staff. Second came the marriage: to one of the brothers (if he was free, and fancied her, or else to a hired Englishman who forthwith disappeared). As the Messinas – by right or wangle

– all held British passports, either served to confer British nationality. A conviction would not then lead to a woman's deportation.

The marriage solemnized and the bride conveyed to London, the pledges given her were generally fulfilled. In Messina fashion. She got the smart address (Bruton Place or Stafford Street); she got expensive garb (tailored skirt, fur stole); she got that equivocal status symbol of our day, a maid. But these were not to be indulged in, not to be enjoyed. These were the quarters and accessories for work. The majority, knowing exactly what awaited them, donned their finery and took to the streets without demur. A minority may have demurred, but just the same took to the streets. They had little choice; the Messinas ruled by terror. Terror of what was threatened. Terror of what was done. They brought terror to the boudoir (as sundry spies discovered). They brought terror to the beat (as I for one observed). They brought terror to intruders, hawking without their licence (as some bold or careless floozies could – but did not – testify). A girl 'known to the police' stabbed to death in a back alley? Another, slit or slugged, alive but saying no word? A pool of blood congealing in the park at daybreak? Some said it, many thought it. 'Must be the Messinas'.

There were no Gang war casualties, however. For a simple reason: there were no Gang wars. No British-based Gang vied with them in size or speciality. Hence, no collective trespass on their territory. Hence, no serious challenge to their influence and control. Sporadic skirmishes with solitary individuals, yes. Pitched battles between big battalions, no. To this extent, the Messinas had the country to themselves. Which makes it no less surprising that they had so long a run without effective interference from above. For more than fifteen years they governed their expanding empire with arrogance, with savagery – and with impunity. For more than fifteen years only one, Eugene, stood trial, and his punishment (three years jail) was for malicious wounding; the Gang's murderous tyranny meanwhile continued unabated. It is difficult to dismiss a strong impression that such a state of affairs could not have persisted unless officials had behaved with culpable inertia. This impression is strengthened further by the fact that the Messinas were at last put out of

OPPOSITE: *The People*, 3 September 1950

32

THE PEOPLE

SUNDAY, SEPTEMBER 3, 1950 No. 3591—69th Year 2d

OVER 4,500,000 SALE

ARREST THESE FOUR MEN

ey are the emperors of a vice npire in the heart of London

' 'The People' has found e facts about a vice ring heart of London that is a national scandal.

● This is an unsavoury story but we believe it is our duty to the public to reveal it so that swift action can be taken.

THE MESSINA GANG EXPOSED

By Duncan Webb

YESTERDAY I made the final entry in a dossier that uncovers the activities of a vice gang operating in the West End of London on a scale that will appal every decent man and woman.

Today I offer Scotland Yard evidence from my dossier that **should enable them to arrest four men who are battening on women of the streets and profiting from their shameful trade.**

And, to support that suggestion, I intend to expose in detail the way in which this gang operates—a story so sordid that I am certain public opinion will now demand that this state of affairs should not be tolerated a moment longer.

The four men I am accusing are brothers, members of what is openly known to the police—and even to Parliament—as The Messina Gang.

Let there be no doubt as to whom I am naming as the members of this gang on these grave charges. The four men are:—

EUGENE MESSINA, who normally calls himself Edward Marshall and who lives at 24, Bruton-place, a mews flat off New Bond-st., Mayfair.

ATTILIO MESSINA, who is usually known as Raymond Maynard and who has been living in a block of flats in Kensington Park Gardens, London, W.11.

CARMELO MESSINA, who has changed his name to Charles Maitland and who lives at 3, Lancaster Lodge, a respectable block of flats in North Kensington.

SALVATORE MESSINA, who has changed his name to Arthur Evans and who lives at Kings Court, Hammersmith, London.

These four brothers are Maltese, and therefore have British nationality. They have been in London for some years and they are now wealthy men.

"Lives of shame"

They are engaged in business as dealers and merchants, and undoubtedly they have made some of their money legitimately.

But, by the most detailed investigation which has taken me and my assistants three months to complete, I have proved that in fact they are controlling a chain of flats used for immoral purposes.

They are emperors of an empire of vice in London's West End.

There are women of the streets who are virtually in their power. Many of these women have come from the Continent to carry on their disgusting business.

And these four men know full well that the wives of some of them are openly taking part in this life of shame.

It is a state of affairs that would disgrace one of the licentious ports of the Middle East. That it should exist in London on this scale is almost incredible.

This newspaper commissioned me to uncover the operations of the Messina Gang as a public duty.

For too long the Messinas have been talked about in high places. But for too long nothing has been done to round them up and put the leaders in a place where they can no longer defame the good name of the capital.

There have been mentions of the Messinas in Parliamentary debates. Their names have cropped up in police court proceedings.

Yet they have gone on battening on the proceeds of vice to the point when they have built up a virtual sense of fear among women of the streets.

Three of these Messina brothers have been in trouble with the police before.

EUGENE MESSINA was born on June 26, 1908, in Alexandria, Egypt.

He was convicted in London in 1947, and sentenced to three years' penal servitude for unlawful wounding.

CARMELO MESSINA has been convicted for bribing a warder while visiting his brother in prison. He got two months.

SALVATORE MESSINA was convicted in Egypt in 1932 for living on immoral earnings and was sentenced to six months imprisonment.

Let me now put on record some of the facts I have uncovered about the despicable side of these men's business interests. I have no intention of affronting public decency by printing in detail the way in which their women conduct their hideous business.

It is enough to say that I have records of what has been observed over long periods to have taken place at flats and other residential premises in the West End of London—places that are owned, rented or leased by one or other of these Messinas.

They are able to flout the law in this way partly because they have operated on the grand scale—strange as that may seem—but also because they have been expert at covering up their tracks.

Take first Eugene Messina. He is a man of many addresses, official and otherwise, and he has built around himself a smoke-screen that is not easy to penetrate.

"I watched"

When he was released from prison some months ago, he gave his official address as 3, Lancaster Lodge, London, W.11, which is also the official address of his brother Carmelo.

But, for rating purposes, he gives to the Westminster City Council the address of 24, Bruton-place, W.1. There he occupies a flat under his real name of Eugene Messina.

Next door is No. 26, Bruton-place, which is rated with No. 28. And the name of the rated occupier of this house is E. Marshall, the second name he commonly employs.

And I can prove that 28, Bruton-place is a house used for immoral purposes. It is frequently

Turn to Page 2

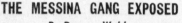

FOUR DESPICABLE BROTHERS

HERE are the four Messina brothers we accuse today.

Top left is Eugene Messina, who calls himself Edward Marshall.

Top right is Carmelo Messina, who has changed his name to Charles Maitland.

Below him is Attilio Messina, who is usually known as Raymond Maynard.

Last of the four in this gallery of despicable brothers is Salvatore Messina, who has changed his name to Arthur Evans.

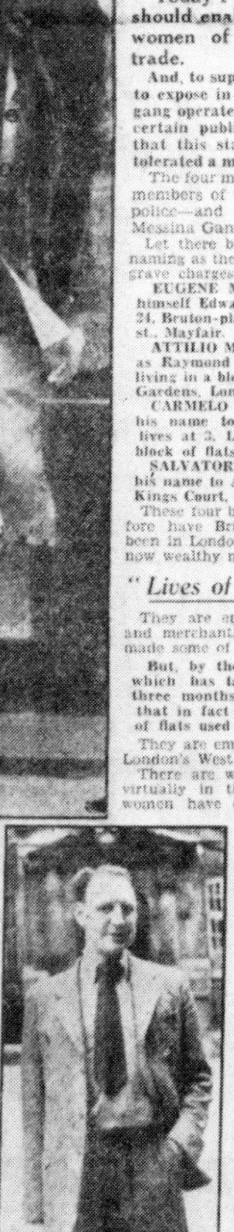

VAS AN RIAGE

n Gilson, e women the Messina

husband, declares r British was born marrying

was paid wedding left him, it was a sentence.

RED TROOPS HALTE IN 'BULGE,' ROUTED IN SOUTH

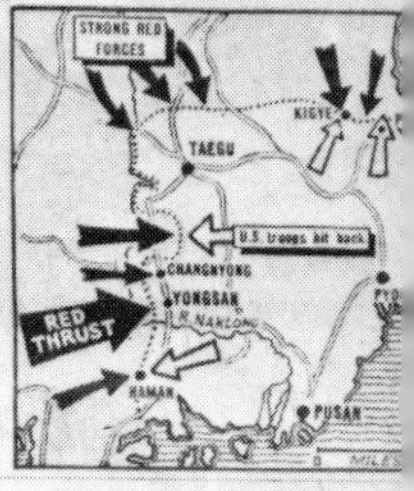

AFTER two days of furious fighting on a 50-mile front, the Communists in Korea have failed to achieve a decisive break-through.

Last night their troops had been brought to a halt at the foothills rising from the plains that form the Naktong River "bulge."

This was their only major penetration—and American reserves, held back until the general picture became clearer, were expected to be hurled into the battle at any moment.

"The position is still fluid but on the way to being stabilised," was the report from General MacArthur's headquarters.

In this central sector, the Reds had advanced eight to ten miles, over flat country that could only have been held by trench warfare.

But last night their attacks were weakening, and their forward units were believed to have lost touch with divisional headquarters.

American tanks and combat engineers yesterday recaptured **YONGSAN**, pivotal town twenty miles north of Masan, and fanned out along the road to Changnyong. This counter-attack may turn out to be the decisive action of the battle.

Further north, the Americans were attacking hills above **WAEGWAN**, and in the extreme south they had pushed two miles beyond battered **HAMAN** in the struggle to protect Masan, main coastal town on the road to Pusan.

Heavy casualties

Light Communist forces got to within five miles of Masan before they were forced back by the U.S. 25th Division, which estimated enemy losses in the southern battle as 10,000 killed and wounded.

The latest U.S. tanks, the 48-ton Pattons, with 90 m.m. guns, went into action for the first time.

"We have retaken all our old positions—Masan has been saved," said a divisional spokesman.

On the east coast Pohang front, the Communists were reported to have captured **KIGYE**, but there was no evidence that the main weight of the Red offensive was likely to be switched to this area. Later, the Americans made rapid progress in a two-pronged attack.

Everywhere the North Koreans suffered heavy casualties. Allied aircraft knocked out twenty-seven tanks.

ATTLEE HITS BACK AT CHURCHILL

MR. ATTLEE, in a party political broadcast, last night replied to the "peremptory demand" of Mr. Churchill for an earlier recall of Parliament, and outlined the reasons he had given the Tory leader for fixing the date for September 12.

"He described my attitude as sullen," said the Prime Minister. "I should describe him as dictatorial.

"For the last 20 years Mr. Churchill seems to me to have regarded Parliament mainly as a place where he makes speeches.

"He comes down like a prima donna, delivers his oration and then, except for an occasional appearance at question time, is seen no more until the next occasion.

"The real work of the House proceeds without his assistance."

Turning to Korea, Mr. Attlee said: "There was no muddle or hesitation. Mr. Churchill knows this quite well, but apparently it's not much good giving him information."

On Craven Brothers' contract with Russia for supplying machine tools, Mr. Attlee said:

"It has never been our policy to set up an iron curtain in trading matters.

"We made a trade agreement with Russia to our mutual benefit. We have since received feeding stuffs and timber in exchange for machinery. They have carried out their side of the bargain and we are carrying out ours."

"Eighteen months ago we took steps to ensure that equipment and tools regarded as of key importance for strategic purposes should not be exported except in the case of contracts already concluded.

"As to inspection, which is not unreasonable in the manufacture of goods of this kind, specific instructions have been given to ensure that it is made in conditions which prevent any disclosure of secrets."

Good Morning People!

IN spite of the rebuff he received last week from President Truman, General MacArthur is still up to his trouble-making tricks. Now he has thought up a new dodge to force the American Government to claim Formosa as a defence bastion in the Far East. He has been trying to convince Washington that Red China was about to intervene in the Korean War. From his headquarters reports were spread that Chinese Communist troops had already crossed the Yalu River, which forms the frontier between China and North Korea.

These reports are untrue. The British Government's latest and most reliable information is that, far from crossing the Yalu, the Chinese are building fortifications on their own side of it! They are simply digging in against a possible backwash of the war.

THIS supports our Foreign Office's confident belief that Red China is, in fact, most anxious to keep the peace. Her internal problems are so urgent that nothing short of open provocation would induce her to give battle.

MacArthur, unchecked, might supply that provocation. That is why Mr. Ernest Bevin, our Foreign Secretary, is eager to meet Mr. Acheson in Washington next week to discuss a plan for the settlement of the whole Formosa question.

'No' to busmen

A WAGE demand by London's 55,000 bus, tram and trolley-bus workers for another £1 a week has not received support from the national executive of the Transport and General Workers' Union.

The executive's decision was communicated privately to the passenger group of the union yesterday.

Pole on the run 'fled British spy school' SAYS MOSCOW

EUGEN STEFANOWICZ, the Pole wanted by Scotland Yard on the Cosy Corner murder and who vanished in a Russian ship in July, escaped "from a British intelligence school for foreigners," Moscow radio declared last night. Since his "escape" he had been "systematically persecuted by the British police," the radio alleged.

Stefanowicz left London in the Russian freighter Sestroretsk and Britain asked Sweden to arrest him, for extradition, when the ship reached Stockholm, but when she arrived there passengers reported that the man had been dumped overboard "like a sack of potatoes" on to a Russian tugboat.

Moscow radio said that Stefanowicz, after serving in the Emigre Polish Army, was sent to Britain.

"On his arrival," the radio went on, "Stefanowicz was sent to a British intelligence school for foreigners which specially trains people to be sent to the Soviet Union and Poland.

"Being unwilling, however, to be a tool of the British Intelligence Service, he escaped from the school, in which connection he began to be systematically persecuted by the British police.

On July 16, Stefanowicz presented himself at the U.S.S.R. Embassy in London and declared that he wanted to be repatriated to the Soviet Union. He was given a certificate.

"According to available information," the radio declared, "Stefanowicz's departure aroused alarm in some British circles, and the whole British Press began to publish items with insinuations against Stefanowicz, even including accusations against him to the effect that, while in Britain, he was guilty of a criminal offence."

The statement added that requests by Britain that Stefanowicz should be handed over had been rejected.

William Dearlove, sixty-eight, proprietor of the "Cosy Corner" café and shop opposite a Polish resettlement at Hazlemere, Bucks, was found strangled.

A Pole, Zbigniew Kalinowski, 22, was sent for trial accused of being concerned "with another person," in the murder.

MORE RAIN

DON'T be deceived bright start to the ... more rain is on its way ... it will not be long in ...

The new wet-weather ... will come in from the ... and by this afternoon ... be cloudy in most ... Heavy showers will ... but the South may ... with light drizzle.

THE TRA... MISSED

HUNDREDS of people gasped as a church ... which was being demo... Southampton, swayed ... railway line along ... London-bound express ... line yesterday, and the... back again and remain...

All trains on the ... main London-Bournemo... were diverted for an ho...

Workmen had put a ... round the 50-ft. tower ... Trinity Church and were ... the hawser in when it ...

Half the tower fell ... half swayed two feet ... line, only a few yards ...

OPPOSITE TOP: In 1956, Eugene Messina was arrested in Belgium on a charge of illegal possession of firearms and attempted procuring. He was sentenced to six years

OPPOSITE BOTTOM: The *Daily Mirror*, 10 April 1959. Attilio Messina found guilty at the Old Bailey

business, not by anyone or anything in duty bound to do so, but by a fearless journalist backed by a crusading paper.

Duncan Webb was a crime reporter on *The People*. He had never seen a single one of the Messinas, but daily in his job encountered indications of their ugly presence and pervasive power. He grew sickened by these foreign occupiers – and by the passive guardians of the occupied. With his editor's sanction and co-operation, he set himself a task that others should have done. In his own words: '*To prove* that the Messinas were an organized Gang purveying vice and corruption for immoral purposes and financial profit.' After months of tireless effort, Webb achieved his aim. On 3 September 1950, *The People* carried a dramatic front page spread: the first of eight articles exposing the Messinas. A true *exposé*. It not merely proclaimed, asserted, and denounced. It gave names, places, dates, and photographs. Using an expression just then popular – the lot.

It hit the public like a gale, the Messinas like a cyclone. They fled abroad, standing not upon the order of their going. Eugene and Carmelo, on the 10th; next, Salvatore; next, Attilio. Only Alfredo braved the blast, and stayed. They can never catch *me*, he boasted to his intimates. He was, it is true, better shielded than the rest. Then aged fifty, he had lived for seven years with a woman named Hermione Hinden at a house in Wembley which he had bought in 1942. Alfredo thus presented a respectable façade. The household? Like a million middle-class *ménages*. Except that, at six o'clock or thereabouts most evenings, the master drove his lady into the West End; drove back, alone, immediately, to Wembley; returned in the small hours to fetch the lady home. Hermione Hinden was in fact a full-time Messina prostitute, with her own demarcation lines, her own *chambre d'amour*, and a hundred and four convictions for soliciting. Alfredo, of course, had not had an inkling of this; it was, of course, a ghastly error or a wicked plot when detectives entered his villa and arrested him. He swore he never knew, never faintly guessed, his constant companion's constant occupation; never demanded, never received, so much as a farthing from her; on the contrary, he kept her and was generous with gifts. Hermione Hinden corroborated her *souteneur*. But, he was asked, had he worked since being in England? He had not.

34

Had he £9,000 split up between three banks? He had. Did he pay into those banks always in cash? He did. It was cash transferred from safe deposit boxes where he had stored the fortune made by him before the war. Where? In Belgium, and other countries. How? Dealing in diamonds – and diamond merchants, said Alfredo, dealt in cash.

The jury were not fooled; they retired for just twelve minutes. The judge was not fooled; he passed the maximum sentence. Alfredo's appeal was dismissed as 'groundless'. Yet two years' imprisonment had to mimic retribution on the brother Webb considered the most evil of the five. Indeed, if Attilio had not set foot again in England and served an incredibly short stretch for a similar offence, the total custodial punishment imposed on the Messinas would not have reached the derisory sum of five years and a half.

Remembering Capone (and adapting Laurence Sterne) one might say that they order this matter better in the United States. However, Capone being kept in mind, one might also say that even there they don't order it nearly well enough.

'SLAVEMASTER' ATTILIO MESSINA GETS FOUR YEARS

By TONY CONYERS

VICE king Attilio Messina, 48, who "enslaved" a woman for ten years, was gaoled at the Old Bailey yesterday for four years.

The woman was said to have enslaved is Mrs. Edna Kallman, 39. The court was told that she worked as a Mayfair prostitute for Messina, and that—

● She earned £40,000 in the ten years and handed it all to Messina.
● She was allowed £7 a week to pay for her hairdresser, telephone and food.
● She was forced by violence and threats to "work" every day of the week, whether she was well or ill.

Messina, otherwise known as Raymond Maynard, pleaded guilty to procuring Mrs. Kallman to become a common prostitute, and to living on the earnings of prostitution.

The story started in 1941 when Messina "picked up" dressmaker Edna Kallman—who was separated from her husband. He gave her a lift in his car.

'Taught Her the Art'

Later they kissed and stood together, and eventually Messina was making Mrs Kallman a lot of money.

Then said Mr Griffith-Jones, as she was "doing the streets" for a time. He used was brought to Messina and she was ordered never to go out.

That was the amount of "subservience," added Mr. Griffith-Jones that Mrs Kallman was raised and subdued that these came those steps—

● She was introduced to another prostitute who was working for Messina.
● After training Mrs. Kallman was taken to the Messina flat in King's-road, Marylebone, and provided with a flat. She "earned" planned for her by Mr. Griffith-Jones.

Mrs Kallman was given "calm" by Messina, said Mr Griffith-Jones.

She was to have no married clients and was paid to talk to anyone of the silence. She was also given a cards to touch in bad clients to her flat. And her maid was

told that, if Mrs. Kallman "remarked on the number of the client" at the end of any time—four or five and could have left, her flat at any time. Mr. Messina also suggested that there was to afraid of other" of other than Mrs Kallman's own maid watched to support the story of her.

Messina, described as an elderly woman, did ten minutes' work on every half-hours-a-day prostitute. Instead of being imprisoned as he was convicted, described by the Recorder, Sir Gerald Dodson.

The Judge said he would recommend to the Home Office that Messina, who, as an Italian subject, should be deported after serving his sentence.

WHAT THE MESSINA SAYS—SEE PAGE TWO.

She Went to the Police

A factor advised Mrs. Kallman to have a month—say. As she and Messina left the surgery she told him that from now on she would not take the clients.

The story came to an end—brazenly, the Judge said—in February this year, continued Mr. Griffith-Jones.

After inquiries when Messina once a police raid at another prostitute at Wigmore-street. As a result of this Messina was arrested Feb 8.

Now back home in her mother flat lives in Earl's-road, was and had her story. Then she would be given over to...

Mr Webb Messina, following Messina, left Mrs

—Then he will have to quit Britain

● Attilio Messina, 48. He was ordered to be deported in 1951 but no other country would take him, the court was told

● Carmelo Messina, 43. He was deported last month and is now in Italy.

> ●You apparently for ten years have made a sumptuous but revolting type of living from the suffering bodies of women you trapped, seduced and reduced to a form of slavery...You have caused great suffering and it is only right and just that you also should suffer●
>
> —The judge, SIR GERALD DODSON, sentencing Messina yesterday

THE FIVE EVIL BROTHERS WHO REIGNED BY TERROR

By TOM TULLETT
Chief of the Mirror Crime Bureau

THE five evil Messina brothers, vice kings in London for more than twenty years, are finally smashed.

They brought organised vice in London to a scale known before only in Chicago.

And they used Chicago methods of terror and fear.

The five are ATTILIO, gaoled yesterday; EUGENE, in gaol in Chicago; SALVATORE and ALFREDO; and CARMELO, who recently departed to Italy.

How did they run their filthy business?

In the beginning they picked up their girls from the Continent, some of them from good families.

Their methods were always the same. They posed as wealthy business men and spoke sincerely of marriage.

Under this promise seduction followed—and then moral degradation. The girls could not get back to their families.

The next move was to put the girls under the tutelage of

a seasoned prostitute. Often a girl would go through a "marriage of convenience" to a stranger who was prepared to give her his name—and nationality—for £16.

Then the vice-peddling brothers would install the girl in a luxury flat and give her a "beat" in Mayfair — twenty yards of pavement.

With the flat went a maid to keep check on the number of customers, and a man, known as a "ponce," to watch the Messina interests.

EARNED £2,600

All the money earned by the girls had to be paid to the brothers. The girls, in return, were housed, clothed, fed and given pocket money.

One girl, "working" in Stafford-street, Mayfair, earned £2,600 in six weeks.

They ran a vice ring in London

easily had a genuine business, so it was difficult to prove they were living on the immoral earnings of prostitutes.

The Messina brothers prepared for a long time. The girls—there were more than a hundred of them at one time—were too scared to talk.

Police who tried to smash the Messinas were hindered by the difficulties of enforcing the vice laws and because the brothers knew "all the answers."

Each of them apparently had a Rolls-Royce. They all went to the best tailors. Their shirts were silk, hand-made and monogrammed.

They paid women who had grown old in prostitution to watch the younger ones and to collect the money.

HELD BY THREATS

The same women brought recruits to the filthy business.

Once any girl who was in the brothers' clutches tried to get away, she was threatened with a "cutting."

Some were tired were marked for life ... and even those were still so frightened that they would not identify their attackers.

But now the income has gone ... the reign of the Messina brothers is broken.

ALFREDO MESSINA

He was mentioned in the trial of Eugene in Belgium in 1956. A Scotland Yard man said Alfredo had served two years for living on immoral earnings.

● Eugene Messina, 57. He is serving a six-year sentence in Belgium for white slavery.

35

ABOVE: Jack Comer, known throughout the London underworld as Jack Spot.

BELOW: Ronald, Reginald and Charles Kray.

Co-existing with the Messinas, and outlasting them, were a few lesser 'gangs' hardly qualifying as Gangs. Most notably, those headed by Jack Spot and Billy Hill. They were unlawful rather than lawless, fixers more than fighters, rarely translating menace into action. They attracted widespread attention only once – a nine days' wonder – when Spot's face was carved in broad daylight in Soho. For the most part, they went noiselessly about, taking pains to avoid rumpus and disturbance. They had not been cast in the Chicago mould. Nor, for that matter, had the Messinas. Such a product first appeared in England when the Spots and Hills were removed or replaced by the Krays.

Any attempt to generalize about the brothers Kray is bedevilled by the fact that they were twins. Assumptions may follow that in this case are unfounded. Without recourse to science or statistics, simply and solely from personal experience, many believe that twins – especially of the same sex – possess an almost supernatural affinity; that their mental processes and emotional reactions make them into carbon copies of each other. Life does provide examples. I could name some. But, as it happens, they do not include the Krays.

Of course Ronnie and Reggie had certain things in common. Physical appearance: until their mid-twenties, when Ronnie's face grew puffy, people really 'couldn't tell the two of them apart' (a fact which they sometimes turned to some advantage in effecting escapes and arranging alibis). Early upbringing: their nursery, their playground, their fount of education, had been the asphalt jungle depths of Bethnal Green, where even infants neither asked nor granted quarter. Adolescent hell raising: they were precocious tearaways, provoking and relishing and revelling in brawls, toting guns at the ripe age of sixteen. At seventeen, they both became professional boxers, the only honest work that either ever did. Called up for National Service, they spent their military careers either in the glasshouse or AWOL. As fugitives, as captives, they sought similar associates, consorting with criminals, inveterate or incipient. They re-entered the civilian world with a fixed resolve to attain, in concert, the commanding heights of crime.

Far more important, though, than these or other likenesses was one fundamental difference between the twins.

Ronnie was a madman. By strictest definition. Once he was certified and held in an asylum; more than once he was put in a strait-jacket. His madness took the form of paranoid schizophrenia – delusions of grandeur in which the deranged person often identifies with some famous figure. There is a tale told of Bonaparte, anxious to inspect conditions in a Paris madhouse, arriving late one night, unescorted, unannounced, imperiously demanding immediate admission. 'And who do you think *you* are?' said the janitor. 'I am Napoleon,' the visitor replied. 'Oh,' said the janitor, opening the gates. 'Come in. We've got ten of you inside already.' Substitute Capone for Napoleon, and Ronnie Kray might well have been one of the ten. He had devoured Capone until Capone had devoured him. No thrill could equal that of being his idol's avatar. While not unmindful of material rewards, Ronnie was in the Gangster game primarily for kicks.

Reggie presented the reverse of the Kray coin. Amoral as his twin, he was absolutely sane. Like Ronnie, he asked himself: What's in it for me? But he gave himself a very different answer. He was a master of, not a slave to, violence, regarding it as a useful means to a desired end. He may sometimes have employed the means with positive enjoyment. A Capone streak ran through his Costello character. He would not, however, risk the end simply for the means. And Reggie was in the Gangster game primarily for profit.

Thus the Krays were engaged in two concurrent conflicts. One visible – as allies. One concealed – as opponents. Furious quarrels erupted privately; Reggie would charge Ronnie with idiotic recklessness, Ronnie would charge Reggie with inglorious timidity. These exchanges never endangered their alliance; they always stood together against the outside world. It cannot be denied, though, that there was a clash of wills, and not infrequently the madman's will prevailed. This is evident from their history.

No such clashes were anticipated, even by themselves, when they embarked upon their first joint venture: the Regal, a seedy billiard hall in Mile End. (By a typical stratagem – organizing shindies that gradually drove ordinary habitués away – they had leased it from the owner at a knockdown rent.) Billiards continued, but now as a screen; they transformed the hall into an *entrepôt* for crooks – and a catchment area for mugs. Ronnie was the magnet, Reggie was the manager. The design evolved has been depicted by John Pearson in *The Profession of Violence*. 'Ronnie would bring the crowds in, Reggie would fleece them. Ronnie would make their "name" for violence, Reggie would market it. When there was a serious fight, they could both still join in.' To that extent, until that time, Mr Pearson's summing up is wholly justified: 'the ideally complementary couple'. They held out the promise (or the threat) of the ideal Gangster partnership.

The 'Firm' (local euphemism for their Gang) was born in the billiard hall, grew up, and spread out. They started operating in the small change of 'protection', and were naturally caught up in territorial disputes. These had formerly been resolved by inconspicuous pressures. The Firm introduced more spectacular solutions. Ronnie soon found an excuse to use his Luger; the wound was not serious but the repercussions were. While Reggie stormed ('One day you'll get us hanged') and – by immense exertions – suppressed the evidence, other mobsters pondered and, both angry and alarmed, felt that guns could only be met with guns. Gang warfare, Chicago style, was coming to the boil when Ronnie –

after another incident where he had put the boot in – received a three year sentence on a charge of GBH (underworld shorthand for 'causing grievous bodily harm').

As a brother, Reggie must have heard that sentence with regret. As a colleague, he may have heard it with relief. He would miss the companion to whom he was devoted. He would find it easier to run the Firm alone. Without the constant fear of Ronnie's crazy impulses, he could pursue a calculated policy, win much larger prizes, take much smaller risks. While Ronnie was inside, Reggie (supported by elder brother Charles) gave the Firm a new look, a new orientation. He turned his back upon their gutter monarchy, and set his sights on high society and showbiz. The medium was gaming, the bait was ritzy clubs – at first in outré, and hence titillating, settings. He opened 'The Double R', first of its kind in the East End; catching West End fancy too, it was a big success.

39

He opened 'The Wellington Way' nearby; it was an even bigger one. These were precursors of, and pacemakers for, 'Esmeralda's Barn' in fashionable Wilton Place; most celebrated and most chic of the Kray casinos. Smooth professional gamblers mixed with stage and film celebrities, peers of the realm with felons in tuxedos. The recipe spelt riches. 'Esmeralda's Barn' yielded each twin £40,000 a year. All seemed headed for prosperity – and peace. Until Ronnie, freed, reappeared on the changed scene.

Reggie was now content. Ronnie was not. Reggie did not hanker after the old life. Ronnie did. Chatting up posh birds, hob-nobbing with swells – all very well, if you liked that sort of thing. As relaxation. But relaxing from what? Where was the excitement, the violence, the *action*? Without it, you cut no ice; you were a nobody, a nothing. Soon Ronnie was cutting ice again; a somebody, a something. It took only two or three relapses into pointless rough stuff to undermine all that had been steadily built up. Reggie's restraining influence progressively diminished, vanishing altogether when – as much by misfortune as misfeasance – he himself was put away for eighteen months. During his absence, Ronnie had himself a ball. He killed the goose that laid the golden eggs in 'Esmeralda's Barn'; his entourage of nubile boys and blatant hoodlums stripped off the veneer and dispersed the clientele. He revived the sordid rackets that had been virtually laid off. He replenished the Firm with new strongarm men and cutthroats. He reloaded, and resumed carrying, his Luger. Reggie returned too late to stop the rot. He gave up the struggle – and the leadership. His loyalty to Ronnie, however, was unswerving. That meant the twins were finally set on a disaster course.

The nature of their march along that course is well exemplified by the two murders for which they are best known.

The first was that of George Cornell, an old antagonist who had lately joined a Gang led by the brothers Richardson. Smaller, less powerful, their Gang did not cover the same area as the Krays. A feud existed, though, that did not terminate – at least for Ronnie – with the Richardsons' arrest. That followed a Gang fight, unconnected with the Krays, but in which an old friend of Ronnie's had been killed. It was

enough. The Richardsons were out of reach, but sub-ordinates were at large. One of them must be made to pay – and must be seen to pay. On an evening in March 1966, Ronnie walked into 'The Blind Beggar' pub in Whitechapel. George Cornell was drinking at the bar. 'Just look who's here,' he said. Ronnie shot him through the head and walked out into the night. Several saw it happen. Nobody talked – then.

The second murderee was Jack McVitie ('Jack the Hat' – his Gang monicker might have come straight out of Damon Runyon). A Gangster's casual handyman, breaking up through drink, he bungled a killing with which Ronnie had entrusted him. Furthermore, he retained some money paid to him in advance. Furthermore, in public he reviled the twins, loudly proclaiming that he was going to shoot them both. Had he been sober, Jack the Hat would not have said it. Being drunk he sowed the wind and reaped the whirlwind. On an evening in October 1967 he was decoyed to a 'party' at a woman's flat; when he arrived, there was no woman and no party – only the Kray twins and some of their plug-uglies. Ronnie had devised and engineered the plot, but stopped short of casting himself as executioner. Not from squeamish-ness. For a less creditable reason. He taunted Reggie, 'I've done my one, and made a job of it.' Seconds later, Reggie had done his.

ABOVE: Charles and Eddie Richardson, whose gang rivalled the Krays', outside their scrap-metal yard in Brixton

41

Justice – although by then crippled as well as blind – prevailed in the end to the fullest extent which the hamstrung law allowed. Today, behind bars, both twins are doing theirs.

And the Mafia?

It is popularly believed that this association, linked by family and marriage, governs – whether indirectly or directly – all Gangs, whenever or wherever they appear. And there is much informed support for that belief. From Kefauver:

RIGHT: During the Krays' trial at the Old Bailey leading witnesses were intimidated

BELOW: The twins are sentenced; *Evening News*, 5 March 1969

45,728   London: Monday September 6 1971   5   3p

Car gangsters shoot twice in Fulham street

LONDON BID TO KILL KRAY CASE WITNESS

SARAH ST. CLAIR, 15: she saw the shooting

Evening News   London Wednesday March 5, 1969

MR. JUSTICE MELFORD STEVENSON TELLS RONALD AND REGINALD KRAY

'Society has earned a rest from your activities'

Ronald Kray   Reginald Kray   Charles Kray

The 10 men sent to jail today

The Kray also sentences at the Old Bailey today were:

RONALD KRAY, aged 35, of Bunhill Row, Clerkenwell; life imprisonment, with the recommendation that he be detained for 30 years.

REGINALD KRAY, aged 35, also of Bunhill Row, Clerkenwell; life, 30 years recommended, and on second charge, 10 years to run concurrently.

JOHN BARRIE, aged 31, of no fixed address; life, 20 years recommended.

RONALD BENDER, aged 30, of Cubitt Town, Poplar; life, 20 years recommended.

ANTHONY LAMBRIANOU, aged 26, of Queensbridge Road, Hackney; life, 15 years recommended.

CHRISTOPHER LAMBRIANOU, aged 28, of Queensbridge Road, Hackney; life, 15 years recommended.

CHARLES KRAY, aged 42, of Ravensfield Gardens, Tower Hamlets; 10 years.

FREDERICK FOREMAN, aged 36, of Lant Street, Southwark; 10 years.

CORNELIUS WHITEHEAD, aged 26, of Ravensfield Gardens, Tower Hamlets; seven years.

ALBERT DONAGHUE, aged 32, of Devons Road, Bow; two years.

John Barrie

Ronald Bender

TWINS: LIFE OR 30 YEARS

By STUART FRIEND, CYRIL LING and MICHAEL McDONOUGH

The Kray twins, Ronald and Reginald, aged 35, were sentenced at the Old Bailey today for murder.

Mr. Justice Melford Stevenson said: I am not going to waste words on you. I sentence you to life imprisonment. In my view society has earned a rest from your activities and I recommend you be detained for 30 years.

The sentences on the Krays are the longest for murder ever imposed at the Old Bailey.

Last of the 10 men sentenced was Albert Donaghue, who had earlier pleaded guilty to being an accessory after the Jack McVitie murder.

Axeman case

Today he admitted plotting in the escape of Frank "Axeman" Mitchell from Dartmoor in 1966, and harbouring him.

Before Donaghue was sentenced to two years, Mr. Jones, prosecuting, talked about Mitchell's escape.

"I am guarded in what I am saying because it is the substance of a future trial," he said. "The prosecution say he has been murdered."

RONALD KRAY, the first man in the dock, grimaced when he heard his sentence.

NIGHTMARE YEARS OF REG KRAY'S WIFE

And as he stepped down from the heavily guarded dock, the hand signalled an — a professional boxer formed his fingers into a quick shape and poked at someone in the crowded public gallery.

The only words he spoke were when Det-Supt Leonard "Nipper" Read, who has headed the investigation into the case, referring to a house in which the Kray twins lived

And brother Charles gets ten years

Charles Kray, 42-year-old brother of the twins, was one of the eight others sentenced by Mr. Justice Melford Stevenson at the Old Bailey today.

He got the maximum sentence he could get for his crime of being an accessory after the murder of McVitie—10 years.

The judge told him: "I may well be that you were not a member of what has been called in this case The Firm.

"But I am satisfied that you were an active and ready helper in the dreadful affair of concealing the traces of the murder that your brothers committed and that you were called in and seconded for that purpose and that you were energetic in carrying out that purpose."

Mr. Justice Melford Stevenson, had urged the judge to take into consideration the fact that Charles was a complete separate case to that of his twin brothers.

Det. Supt. Read, after giving convicting evidence on the Old Bailey man, Mr. J. Hazan, told the jury that Charles Kray had one grinding conviction for an offence which was not concerned with the present inquiries.

He was an ex-Naval man, discharged for health reasons but later became a professional

CONVICTION

Bouquet of tulips from the jury

The last function of the Old Bailey jury was to present Mrs. J. Hazan, with a bouquet of tulips. According to 11 it was a nice expression the supposition.

Mr. Hazan said: "Look how after them and making sure they did not go so sick we lost much of our life.

"Each juror has earned his rest and their impression of old-Mac-Ba in my support, and afterwards whenever anyone felt off-colour they came to me."

INSIDE NEWS

WE MAY HIT BACK, NIXON WARNS HO—Page Two

OLYMPIC BOXER IN COURT—Page Five

GLC HOME LOAN RATE JUMPS TO A NEW HIGH—Page Five

GOOD RATES NEWS FOR $7,000—Page Eleven

DOCTORS GET TOUGH WITH THE BOSSES—Page Eleven

DR. FINLAY'S WIFE GETS DEGREE—Page Eleven

FLU SCARE HITS ARSENAL—Back Page

FIRST WITH THE NEW. RING 353 6000 (STD code 01)

Heath ill

Tory leader Mr Heath had a temperature today following an inoculation for his Middle East trip at Easter. He was unable to open the second day of the Conservative defence debate.

Pothole squad

Because so many potholes have appeared in Kensington roads, a special squad of Council workmen have been switched to carry out repairs.

'Behind the local mobs which make up the national crime syndicate is a shadowy, international, organization known as the Mafia.' From Ernest Millen, formerly Commander of the CID and Deputy Commissioner at the Yard: 'It is ... spreading its network of control over the whole world.' Capone (says Kobler, his biographer) 'maintained liaison' with it. The brothers Kray (says Pearson, their biographer) had a 'working agreement' with it. Clearly, in even a brief account of Gangs and Gangsters, at least a footnote on the Mafia is required.

Originally it was a league of peasants, formed early in the nineteenth century, to resist oppression and extortion by land owners in Sicily. First infiltrated, then engulfed, by villains, they soon became far worse oppressors and extortioners (adding murder, brigandage and rape) than those whom they nominally opposed. It was this metamorphosed Mafia which – through the Great Migration – reached out abroad.

A secret society at home, elsewhere they preserved their character as such with rigour. In America, where the majority congregated, for years none were admitted to their ranks except Sicilians; only an internal revolution, marked by corpses, made affiliation open to mainland Italians. And even if exclusiveness has been still more reduced, secrecy has been if anything increased. That is what makes it – an intended consequence – so hard to define the extent of Mafia power. One racketeer, subpoened by the Senate Crime Committee, said that in Sicily itself the Mafia is not discussed. Another, asked if he knew what the Mafia was, said that he didn't, that he had never heard the word. To say that they keep mum about themselves would be inadequate. They go further – or not so far. They deny their own existence.

I once told a witty woman that I was going to speak at a gathering of Masons. 'How do they know that they are Masons?' she asked. 'I thought it was a secret.'

And the Mafia?

2.

CITY CASES

Whitaker Wright
Lord Kylsant
Clarence Hatry
Horatio Bottomley
the Lynskey Tribunal
Ferdinand Lesseps
Teapot Dome

These are the cases which arise from what, according to Lady Bracknell, the radical papers call the purple of commerce. Cases which are full of words like flotation, capitalization, collateral, par value. Cases which generally receive more coverage in *The Times* than in the *News of the World*. Cases which, it is argued, should be tried by a panel of experts, because ordinary citizens can never understand them. Wherever they occur, they are still labelled City cases – a reminder of the days when the City (of London) was both the symbol and the hub of high finance.

City cases, as a class, seldom excite the interest of those who follow crime for drama, for sensation. It is assumed that they are deficient in those two ingredients. Experience and example, though, invalidate that assumption. Their subject matter may be coldly arithmetical, but the situations they create often stir the pulse. What could be more dramatic (melodramatic, even) than that of the tycoon who has entered his gleaming Rolls at the front door of the Ritz and alights from it at the back door of the Old Bailey? What could be more sensational (shocking, even) than his presence between warders in that celebrated dock, occupied yesterday by a murderer, tomorrow by a burglar or rapist? And how many trials for murder or burglary or rape end with the accused committing suicide in court? As at least one of the accused did in a City case.

His name was Whitaker Wright.

W.W. – the initials once were as familiar as L.G. or W.G. – was the very model of a self-made man. Born without advantages of family or education, he set off as a penniless youth for the United States, returning to England at the age of forty-four with a fortune amassed on the New York Stock Exchange. He lived in grandeur consonant with his wealth; peacocks on the terrace, Leonardos on the wall. But he was not content to lounge in idle luxury, simply enjoying the fruits of his earlier endeavours. He took to company promotion in the largest way, multiplying his own fortune and, in many instances, making that of others. He was a wizard, that is to say, a successful gambler. He was also a manipulator, that is to say, a crook – and, in due course, the day of reckoning came.

PAGE 44: Clarence Hatry

The nature and form of W.W.'s crookedness were notable less for originality than scale. He did what other swindlers had done and were to do. He switched funds from one company to another, and back again, as ingenuity prompted and expediency required. Such switches were not always disclosed (sufficiently or at all) to shareholders (existing or potential). Thus the available figures worked like a distorting mirror. They failed to reflect the true condition of the companies. High dividends, however, diverted or postponed suspicion until the parent company (London and Globe) collapsed. W.W. then was charged with publishing false balance sheets. He absconded to America, was traced and extradited, and was put up to plead – Not Guilty – in January 1904.

In retrospect, his guilt is manifest. In prospect, his conviction appeared far from certain. So much so that the

LEFT: Whitaker Wright

47

Attorney-General (Robert Finlay) refused to authorize a public prosecution. It was a consortium of aggrieved and injured individuals which had launched, and which pursued, the criminal proceedings. That fact in itself greatly aided the defence. A *private* prosecution? The term has nasty nuances, inviting exploitation by a skilled defender. It suggests – or can be projected to suggest – personal spite employing the law as an instrument, on evidence deemed insufficient by detached officials. But something else favoured W.W. even more: the sheer complexity of the challenged operations. This may explain the Attorney-General's inaction. Comprehensible to me, one can imagine Finlay thinking, but will it be so to untrained minds ignorant of big business? The butcher and the baker in the jury box – will they not find the whole affair a hopeless muddle? And if they do, and if the muddle can't be sorted out, will they not give the prisoner the benefit of the doubt?

If this was Finlay's reasoning, as I tend to believe, the result of the trial did not really vitiate it. The butcher and baker apparently did understand – but only because of flawless exposition from the Bar coupled with illuminating guidance from the Bench. Once they understood, their verdict was ordained. So W.W. could count himself twice over unlucky. With his prosecutor. And with his judge.

Rufus Isaacs was one of the very greatest advocates who has ever practised in the English courts, ranking among that immortal band of Titans which includes Russell, Clarke, Carson, Hastings, Birkett (though not, despite popular opinion, Marshall Hall). Like the rest, Isaacs excelled in eloquence, in personality, in cross-examination. But he had individual gifts which might have been implanted for the purpose of bringing W.W. to book. First, he had a wonderful ability to simplify, to impose order upon chaos, to translate esoteric jargon into common speech. Second, he had a head for figures as some have a head for heights; he could 'read' at a glance a profit-and-loss account or balance sheet – not merely a matter of addition and subtraction, but of spotting the relevant items (and omissions). Third, he was fully acquainted with commercial processes; had himself been 'in the City' before entering the law; could not be blinded with science – or with daybooks or with ledgers. Isaacs used all these three gifts to sketch a background with which the jury felt familiar and at home by the time he came to interrogate W.W.

His Lordship contributed some brush strokes to the background, and some questions to the interrogation. Not by way of prejudice; rather for reinforcement. As one typical passage demonstrates.

Isaacs was asking about the Annual General Meeting.

'You knew then that there were rumours circulating?'

'No doubt.'

'You were anxious to put the best face on the Globe's affairs?'

'No doubt.'

'You knew that the important matter to the shareholders was the sum of £2,332,000 declared to be held by Globe in sundry companies?'

'The state of the Company was the important thing.'

An oblique, evasive, answer. As the judge would note. For Mr Justice Bigham, too, was a renowned commercial lawyer who knew every move in the game of Lothbury noughts and crosses.

'£2,332,000.' Isaacs lingered over the repetition. 'It was important to know, wasn't it, how much had been written off?'

'Yes.'

'You said over one million pounds had been written off. For depreciation. That was untrue?'

'I do not admit it was,' W.W. rejoined. 'You must take the whole together.'

'But you *said*,' Isaacs quietly insisted, 'that one million pounds had been written off for depreciation.'

'I should have said *loss* and depreciation. It was an extempore utterance.'

'And totally untrue?'

Neither assent nor contradiction. Isaacs went on to allege that, by juggling with paper transactions, W.W. had 'written up' the value of Globe's assets. The judge elaborated and spelt out the allegations – less for the witness's sake than for the jury's.

'In 1899, you had £500,000 for "contingencies". In 1900, that was put to credit?'

'That's how it would come out,' W.W. had to agree.

The trial spread over two full weeks. At the start, everything was shrouded in thick fog, but a hard white light had slowly penetrated, until at the end the fraud stood out for all the world to see. Isaacs knew it. Bigham knew it. W.W. knew it – and on the last day he came into court prepared. With a tablet secreted in his mouth which, when sentence of seven years was passed, he swallowed.

The tablet contained cyanide of potassium. Twenty minutes later, W.W. was dead.

A theatrical gesture, some would say a brave one. All surely would say a self-inflicted penalty disproportionate to the crime. It may be asked, too, why W.W. alone? Why was no one else brought in to face the music? Were there no co-directors of Globe? And its associates?

Of course there were – but as managing director, W.W. ruled his companies autocratically. The other members of the boards exercised no power, mostly had no real idea of what was going on. The Duke of This, the Earl of That – they were ornamental cyphers enlisted solely for their resounding names. As directors with titles often are. The City expressively calls them guinea pigs. And the presumption of innocence protecting guinea pigs is, *de facto*, almost as strong as that protecting infants.

Two generations after Whitaker Wright, however, a titled director did stand trial in a City case. But the circumstances must be carefully distinguished. Lord Kylsant was not, by the most stringent tests, a guinea pig. His peerage was not even inherited; it crowned a career of public service in and out of Parliament. As chairman of the Royal Mail Steam Packet Company – which owned one of the largest shipping lines in Britain – he was no pompous puppet signing on dotted lines, no fancy figurehead delivering ghosted speeches. His were the brains and energy that made the company tick. Kylsant was Royal Mail and Royal Mail was Kylsant. He took the initatives, and – when things went wrong – the rap.

Like W.W., Kylsant ran into trouble over balance sheets, although it was trouble of quite a different kind. During the First World War, Royal Mail's business boomed; and, with an eye to tax demands as yet unformulated, a large slice of

profits was put into reserve. After the war, when all tax liabilities had been met, still a sum of over £4,000,000 remained; and, as lean years followed the fat, portions of this surplus were from time to time put back into profit. The company thus declared (and paid dividends on) a profit when it was currently running at a loss. 1926, for instance: Trading loss, £300,000; Profit shown, £400,000 – thanks to £700,000 transferred from reserve. The balance sheet did not record this transfer with precision. It did, though, qualify the profit figure thus: 'Including adjustment of taxation reserves'. That, in the Treasury's view, was not good enough; the balance sheet – like that of W.W.'s Globe – failed to reflect the true condition of Royal Mail. So Royal Mail's respected chairman was accused of fraud. And so was Royal Mail's respected auditor.

In that year of 1931, when they were tried, both men were approaching seventy. Each seemed a more appropriate candidate for the Lord Mayor's Banquet than the Central Criminal Court. Lord Kylsant – attired in magnate's uniform of frock coat, high collar, black stock and white slip – was a former president of the London Chamber of Commerce and of the Chamber of Shipping of the United Kingdom. His fellow-defendant, Harold Morland – equally dignified, if less picturesque – had been for years a partner in a firm of accountants known by name to millions who do not know any other. Standing side by side as the clerk read the indictment ('Which you knew to be false. . . . With intent to deceive. . . .'), they personified, as few have done before or since, the peculiar tragedy that can attend a City case. Tell it not in Gath. Nor in London Wall.

BELOW: Sir Patrick Hastings, counsel in the Kylsant case

So far as the balance sheets were concerned, everything turned on those five words: 'Including adjustment of taxation reserves'. They had been inserted personally by Morland, whose defence was that they were common form, in general use and acknowledged by accountants as sufficient indication of a transfer such as Royal Mail's (which, in itself, at that time indisputably was legal). Kylsant's defence was that he had been entitled to rely on the advice and phraseology of his eminent accountant. After a trial lasting nearly as long as Whitaker Wright's (and even more glittering with fashionable counsel – Sir William Jowitt, Sir John Simon, Sir Patrick Hastings), the jury found the balance sheets free from taint of fraud, and Morland was accordingly discharged. But a restraining hand still lay upon Lord Kylsant. For he had been further charged with issuing a false prospectus – false, it was alleged, in virtually the same respect. On that further charge, the jury found him guilty, and the judge imposed twelve months imprisonment. An outcome which is hard to contemplate with satisfaction.

I am more disposed to sympathize with the sufferings of victims than to bewail the punishment of criminals. But nothing persuades me that Lord Kylsant was a criminal. The Crown, in my opinion, never came near proving the basic element of criminality. Intent.

Why, then, did a jury unanimously convict, and a judge indirectly approbate the verdict?

Because of the general attitude that prevailed towards 'the City' – a sequel to the Hatry slump of 1929.

After an ample interval for second thoughts, Clarence Hatry – by uninformed consensus – remains the demon king of English City cases. Though few now remember it, there still vaguely echoes what Mr Justice Avory said when imposing on him the maximum sentence (fourteen years penal servitude): 'The most appalling frauds that have ever disfigured the commercial reputation of this country.' That comment – about the frauds – is not wholly accurate, like the myth about the man which they assisted to engender.

Hatry was not an adventurer, not by preference a rogue, not by temperament an egomaniac. On the first head, he differs from W.W., on the second from Bottomley, on the

53

third from both. He was a financier of unusual acumen who, for many years, ran a group of companies with perfect propriety and advantage to the shareholders. He possessed great dynamic and considerable vision; in our days he would have been described as a whiz-kid. Until he reached forty, success had monotonously followed on success. Then his group encountered what are now known by the euphemism of 'liquidity problems'. More bluntly, they were broke.

Simply to tide over for a few weeks or months – so he hoped, so he anticipated – Hatry adopted, at a partner's prompting, a device which was dishonest and dangerous and thus doubly out of character. He issued, as security for bank loans, additional bearer scrip certificates, intending that the duplicate stock should be redeemed on the completion of a merger then impending. Soon, though, there were too many

OPPOSITE: The *Daily Mirror*, 25 January 1930.

BELOW: Mrs Hatry arriving at court during her husband's trial.

JUDGE AND "MOST APPALLING FRAUDS"

FREE HAMPERS WINNERS' NAMES

Daily Mirror

THE DAILY PICTURE PAPER WITH THE LARGEST NET SALE

No. 8,171   Registered at the G.P.O. as a Newspaper.   SATURDAY, JANUARY 25, 1930   One Penny

2 READERS SHARE £500 PRIZE

HATRY SENTENCED TO 14 YEARS

Clarence C. Hatry, who was sentenced yesterday to fourteen years' penal servitude, photographed with his wife in a schooner.

Edmund Daniels, sentenced to seven years' penal servitude.

John G. G. Dixon, who is to serve 5 years' penal servitude.

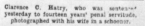

Mr. Justice Avory, who passed the sentences. The trial lasted five days.

Albert Edward Tabor, sentenced to three years' penal servitude.

John Gialdini, who, said Hatry's counsel, suggested the duplication of stock.

Hatry's house in Stanhope-street, W., which is to be sold.

The luxurious main hall of Hatry's house.

In passing sentence on Hatry at the Old Bailey yesterday Mr. Justice Avory remarked: "You stand convicted of the most appalling frauds that have ever disfigured the commercial reputation of this country—frauds far more serious than any of the great frauds on the public which have been committed within the last fifty years, according to my personal experience." Other sentences, to run concurrently with the principal sentences, were passed on all the accused on other counts. Hatry, a picture of sartorial perfection, remained outwardly calm during the Judge's scathing remarks. When he heard the sentence he closed his eyes for a moment.

certificates around. The Stock Exchange suspended dealings in the shares of Hatry's principal company, Austin Friars Trust. An independent computation placed it in the red to the tune of fifteen million pounds. Austin Friars was put into compulsory liquidation; shares in other companies (not only Hatry's) were marked down; something akin to panic was sweeping through the City as Hatry was arrested with four of his close colleagues.

Hatry made no money for himself out of this trick. It was never planned nor supposed that he would do so. The object was to protect the companies – and, as a natural consequence, the investors. His counsel later said: 'Hatry pledged his liberty and reputation and everything that made life worth living so that he might save from ultimate loss a great many innocent people.' Pitching it rather high – but Norman Birkett was making then a speech in mitigation. The judge dismissed the excuse as comparable with that of 'any clerk or servant who robs his master and says that he hoped to repay by backing a winner before his crime was discovered'. One need not accept the exactitude of that analogy to recognize that Hatry had no viable defence. Indeed, at the end of the prosecution's evidence, he withdrew his plea of Not Guilty – on the advice of his defender. Notwithstanding Avory's draconian severity, Birkett's advice was unquestionably wise. Persisting would only have prolonged the agony.

More relevant for us, though, than Hatry's personal fate are the side-effects of the catastrophe. Many suffered grievously from his misdoings; many mistakenly believed that they had done – simple folk, bewildered by the falling market as the repercussions of the Wall Street crash struck here. Nationwide suspicion of 'the City', always latent, temporarily grew into fierce antipathy. Every act of high finance was *ipso facto* crime, every high financier *per se* a criminal. People recoiled from the unacceptable face of capitalism long before that expression had been coined.

Juries, even judges, are not insusceptible to the atmosphere prevailing outside court. Amid the prejudices of the post-Hatry period, Kylsant stood about as much chance of going free as a man in nun's robe and military boots, speaking broken English with a guttural accent, prowling, during the Dunkirk summer, round Biggin Hill.

Hatry was a City man who went wrong. Bottomley was a wrong 'un who went into the City. With a talent as versatile as any that has scrawled a flashy signature across a page of history, this remarkable product of a philanthropic orphanage is remembered in one or more of several roles – according to the interest and age of those remembering.

During the first quarter of this century, there cannot have been a man or woman in the British Isles who had not heard of Horatio Bottomley. He came at you, so to speak, from every direction; every hoarding, every mouth – not least his own. As a spellbinding orator in the House of Commons, still more on the platform, he was second only to, if not the equal of, Lloyd George. As a combative editor and trenchant journalist, he had no rivals whatever, only imitators. As a lay advocate (a Litigant in Person, or an accused conducting his own defence), he could hold his own and stand comparison with the top professionals. Like Goldsmith, he touched nothing he did not adorn. Unlike Goldsmith, he touched nothing he did not also defile. He could never resist the temptation to earn a dishonest penny – a temptation besetting his role as a financier most of all.

Bottomley early began flirting with the City. Before he was twenty-six he had founded several newspapers; mostly local, mostly ephemeral, but also – incredible as it may now appear – that subsequent establishment pillar, *The Financial Times*. He formed a parent company for these, and made it the groundwork of a more ambitious combine. The Hansard Union, with Bottomley as operative boss, with a capital of £500,000, with 'name' directors calculated to inspire confidence (the chairman was none other than the Lord Mayor of London), prospered superficially for a while, during which Bottomley drew huge sums for himself. But the prosperity was factitious and fictitious. Stage by stage the disturbing truth emerged that the gaily decorated ship was on the rocks. Debentures had to be issued in order to pay dividends; the holders, 'turning nasty', seized the Company's premises; Bottomley filed a bankruptcy petition; he and three others (one the ex-Lord Mayor) were charged with conspiracy to defraud.

The case threatened to end his career in high finance. Instead it launched his career as a lay advocate.

The other defendants instructed leading counsel. Bottomley decided to defend himself. An unorthodox decision, all the more audacious as the Attorney-General would be prosecuting and, in 1893, the Attorney-General was Charles Russell (whose very presence caused stout hearts to palpitate and veteran knees to knock). More audacious still as the judge was to be Mr Justice Hawkins, outstanding scourge of criminals – and, often, witnesses. Bottomley, of course, had nimble wits and a glib tongue, but his sole vocational training for this formidable occasion had been haphazard and almost juvenile. First, as an office boy to shady solicitors; second, as an official shorthand reporter, observing the methods of the barristers he reported.

Despite – or because of – this singular apprenticeship, Bottomley's performance was a *tour de force*. His self-assurance and continuous effrontery, mixed with a proprietory brand of wheedling, paid off. Spectators wearing wigs grown grey in service watched and listened admiringly,

BELOW: Horatio Bottomley addressing a recruitment rally in Trafalgar Square, August 1915

agape. Not only that; he secured his own acquittal. Not only that; he contributed more than anyone towards the acquittal of his co-defendants. Not only that: after the trial Hawkins sent for him and privately advised him to chance his fortunes by going to the Bar.

Bottomley did not do so. He was in a hurry, and had other fish to fry. But the Hansard Union convinced him, not without good reason, that few, if any, in the Temple surpassed his forensic powers. Henceforth he eagerly grasped at opportunities to display them. Often he created such opportunities, mostly through his favoured medium, the provocatively written and widely read *John Bull*. Writs for libel flowed into that journal's office and Bottomley welcomed them as a fledgling in chambers welcomes briefs. He avoided settlements – even sensible settlements – when he could. He relished too much the *réclame* and excitement of his spectacular and frequently successful exhibitions.

It was in accordance with classical unities that the courts, which had been the setting for Bottomley's greatest triumphs were also the setting for his irreparable ruin. That, which occurred in 1922, arose out of what was called the Victory Bond Club.

During the years since the Hansard Union, Bottomley had been intensely active in many spheres. Most prominently, perhaps, in the First World War as (paid) booster of national morale (attracting, incidentally, more recruits into the forces than all the famous posters of Kitchener's pointing hand). Most consistently, perhaps, back in the City jungle, where, burnt fingers quickly healed with golden ointment, he promoted all sorts of companies. One of these was the Joint Stock Trust and Finance Corporation which involved him in another conspiracy charge (on which he was cleared by the efforts of the same defender whom he had employed with such good effect before).

In the Victory Bond Club, Bottomley combined the arts of a patriotic propagandist and a conman.

War loans, however packaged, had long been represented – not least by Bottomley in his subsidised harangues – as both support for Britain and a paying line for Britons. (Some today might dispute the latter proposition.) Cheap issues, like savings certificates at 15s 6d, went well, at least while the thunder of the guns could be heard across the Channel. But in 1919, with £5 Victory Bonds, the Government priced itself out of the market. And yet the twin inducements, moral and material, appealed. Bottomley detected, and utilized, the opening. The Victory Bond Club (successor in form to his earlier War Stock Combination) offered one fifth of a Victory Bond for £1 down. 'I will buy Bonds,' Bottomley proclaimed, 'hand them over to trustees, and each year we will draw for the accruing interest.' Investors were assured that they could withdraw their capital in full at any time.

Such expectations, though, were unfulfilled. The public did their part; money poured in. But Bottomley did not appoint any trustees, and the mounting number asking for their money back didn't get it, or only got it after much delay. That was due to a variety of causes, some beyond Bottomley's immediate control (forged vouchers, dishonest employees). But the root of the trouble was the old rogue himself, and the outcry rightly concentrated on him.

Two voices picked themselves out above the din. Both articulate, menacing – but very different. One was that of the weekly journal, *Truth*, which repeatedly criticized the 'so-called' Club in fastidious prose. The other was that of a man named Reuben Bigland, who stigmatized Bottomley explicitly and crudely ('One of the greatest crooks ever born') in a pamphlet widely distributed by hand. Bottomley issued a few writs against *Truth*, but, when they were ignored, apparently did not press them. Against Bigland, however, he committed himself more deeply. He set in motion the criminal law.

There was an ambiguous relationship between Bottomley and Bigland. From time to time they were associated in fraud; then Bottomley had no devotee more loyal. From time to time, Bigland yielded to conscience and repented (or felt dissatisfied with the division of the spoils); then Bottomley had no enemy more bitter. Prosecuted for libel (with blackmail charges thrown in for good measure), Bigland behaved like the vicious animal of fable: *quand on l'attaque, il se défend.* Moreover, his *défense* was itself an *attaque*. In the upshot, Bottomley was on trial as much as Bigland.

The former spent four uncomfortable days before the senior Bow Street Magistrate. Bigland's counsel, Comyns

ABOVE: Bottomley
leaving the Bow Street
court, 1921

Carr, raked him with probing questions; Bottomley, wielding
a blade now tempered in many fires, was restricted in its use
by a painful consciousness that he, the self-appointed guardian of the Little Man, had plundered the Little Man's (and
the Little Woman's) funds. In this opening match, Bigland
had the best of the play. Bottomley, though, achieved the
result which he had sought. Bigland was sent for trial – to the
Old Bailey for libel, to Shropshire Assizes for blackmail,
according to where the respective offences were allegedly
committed.

The Old Bailey hearing came on first, in January. Bigland
had entered a plea of 'justification', that is, that what he had
written about Bottomley was true. He filed in support more
than fifty specific statements, most, if not all, of which
Bottomley must have known could be substantiated. The
prosecutor was represented now by Marshall Hall, who, after
strenuously applying for an adjournment – opposed by
Comyns Carr, rejected by the judge – announced forthwith
that he would offer no evidence. Which meant that Bigland,
though formally acquitted, had no opportunity to ventilate
his plea in open court. Which also meant that Bottomley had
thrown in his hand.

Less than a month later, at Shropshire Assizes, Bigland won the second match, and thereby ensured the third. Bottomley handed him the decision by default – with even more conspicuous dishonour than before. Bigland described in detail some of Bottomley's swindles to which he himself ('to my shame and sorrow') had been party. And Bottomley, present in court, did not go into the box. 'When all this has been given in evidence,' the judge said to the jury, 'what do you think of Mr Bottomley remaining silent?' The jury took only a minute or two to agree on what they thought, and expressed it in the only way they could.

Bigland's acquittal could be equated with Bottomley's conviction. The official stamp upon it was not long delayed. In May, Bottomley again appeared at the Old Bailey. This time without Marshall Hall, this time in the dock, charged with fraudulent appropriation of sums totalling £170,000. He defended himself with not much less than his old dexterity, and rather more of his old histrionics: 'The sword of justice would drop from its scabbard if you gave a verdict of Guilty against me.' But even he, the most irrational of optimists, must have realized that his task was absolutely hopeless as Travers Humphreys, prosecuting without flourishes, drove

RIGHT: Bottomley after his release from prison

him, item by item, into admission that (I quote Alan Hyman's *The Rise and Fall of Horatio Bottomley*) 'all the amounts mentioned in the indictment had been drawn for his own purposes,' even though he maintained that 'these amounts were owing to him as he had advanced large sums to the [Victory Bond] Club.'

Bottomley went down for seven years. He was granted two years remission for 'good conduct' as a prisoner. He came out full of schemes for re-establishing himself – schemes destined never to reach fruition. His flair as a journalist had deserted him. His oratorical gifts were either denied an outlet, or projected in uncongenial conditions where they failed. The gates of the City, of course, were for ever closed against its most colourful, if not its greatest, scamp.

Bottomley was an MP. His disgrace rubbed off on Parliament. Politicians as a class suffered in esteem. Not, however, in such degree as to threaten institutions. It is different when senior ministers, senior State functionaries, are linked, however tenuously, with a City scandal. The machinery of Government then may fall under suspicion.

English history has been relatively exempt from such unsavoury and perilous episodes. It looked, though, as if one were brewing in 1948 when a resolution of both Houses called for an inquiry into 'allegations that payment, rewards, or other considerations have been sought, offered, promised, made or received by or to Ministers of the Crown or other public servants in connection with licences or permissions . . . .' Among those subjected to investigation was the Minister of Works and a director of the Bank of England. If heads like theirs had rolled, the results would have been incalculable. But the Lynskey Tribunal – the name deriving from the High Court judge who was its chairman – wreaked no devastating havoc in high places. Its most dramatic instant consequence was to end the public career of an obscure under-secretary and return him to his avocation of a railway clerk.

The Lynskey Tribunal's long term significance, indeed, does not concern directly either Whitehall or the City. It concerns go-betweens and channels of communication. The Tribunal spotlighted the penetration into our business fabric of the Fixer.

The Second World War (and its immediate aftermath) was a natural forcing bed for this phenomenon. Want to import? Export? Need materials? Supplies? Tied up by red tape? Leave it to me, I'll fix it. Scores of characters appeared thus willing to oblige, but only one became an international figure, for a while sharing the headlines with Stalin and Truman and Marlene Dietrich and Manchester United. Stanley *né* Kohyzcky, Stanley formerly Rechtand, Stanley the star witness of the Lynskey Tribunal.

BELOW: Sidney Stanley, principal figure in the Lynskey Tribunal, December 1948

Who is *principal* witness in a case depends on circumstances. Who is *star* witness depends on personality, on the subjective power to attract (for good or ill) the lion's share of interest. Stanley achieved this partially by his background, which suggests a tale written in collaboration by Peter Cheyney, E. Phillips Oppenheim and Dumas. A background of sumptuous living (Park Lane flat, plush limousines); of mountainous finance ('£400? Chicken feed!'); of enormous, perpetual, and plausible volubility (especially on phone calls to Government departments); of prodigal entertainment in expensive restaurants; of lavish and confident claims – occasionally well-founded, invariably convincing – to intimate associations and friendship with the great. 'He talks,' someone said, 'as if he knew everyone except His Majesty – and would probably put him in, too, if he were pressed.' Talking with nonchalant indifference in millions, talking with ease to ex-directory subscribers, Sidney Stanley represented the apotheosis of a work-shy generation – the top Contact Man.

ABOVE: Sir Hartley Shawcross, the Attorney-General, arrives at Church Hall, Westminster, for a hearing of the Lynskey Tribunal

65

And his background comprised only a quarter of the secret. Three-quarters of it lay right in the foreground, in his performance at the Tribunal itself. Even the most blameless – and most resilient – might have been somewhat battered and exhausted after fifteen hours of questioning by Sir Hartley Shawcross who, as Attorney-General, was not only titular leader of the Bar, but also its leader by capacity and talent. Coolly and expertly and relentlessly, Shawcross explored one dubious corner after another of Sidney Stanley's past activities, and at the end, these had been nakedly revealed.

But so had Stanley's peculiar native quality. He was not battered, he was not exhausted. Overflowing with humour and limitless panache (a sort of genial megalomaniac), he loomed twice as large as life and ten times as bizarre. It may fairly be said that Stanley was exposed. It cannot fairly be said that he was crushed. To compare his buoyancy with that of a cork would flatter corks.

Shawcross asked him: 'Up to the outbreak of war, were you acting generally as a commission agent?'

'Yes.'

'Right through the war, you acted as a commission agent to promote contracts?'

'I would not say *promote*.'

'Assisting?'

'Yes – assisting and completing contracts.'

'Mainly in the clothing trade?'

'*Only* in the clothing trade.'

'After the war, did you continue in these activities?'

'No.'

'What did you change to?'

'Buying and selling stores.'

'Buying and selling *what*?'

'Stores.' Stanley waved his arms expansively. 'Stores, stores – departmental stores.'

'You changed' – Shawcross poker-faced and poker-voiced – 'from selling dresses to selling departmental stores?'

Stanley followed up enthusiastically.

'When you say selling dresses, I was never interested in selling ten or twenty dresses. I always sold thousands – thousands.'

Shawcross asked him: 'Did you introduce this director of the Bank of England to persons in the business world?'

'I did. He had come to me, and said "We're in trouble in the export." So I introduced him to the biggest export people in the country.'

'Specifically, to whom?'

'I introduced him to one gentleman with a turnover of sixty million pounds a year.'

'Might we have his name?'

'I think I ought to write his name,' Stanley said demurely, as if a sixty-million turnover was a statutory offence.

'Don't be so shy, Mr Stanley,' Shawcross exhorted him.

'I am not so shy. But I don't want to bring in innocent people who are trying to help their country.'

Shawcross asked him: 'Is it a usual method of business giving boxes of cigars, bottles of whisky and so on to those with whom you have to conduct commercial negotiations?'

'Certainly.'

'It eases the way?'

'I agree.'

'There is nothing wrong in doing that?'

'Nothing whatsoever.'

'With business associates?'

'Nothing wrong whatsoever.'

'Or with Government officials or ministers?'

'It depends.'

'On the type of person he is?'

'Oh no, no, no, no. Let me tell you, Mr Attorney, that I gave twenty cigars to Mr Bevin [the Foreign Secretary], and he saw nothing wrong in it. I didn't ask him to declare war on anybody.'

The Lynskey Tribunal uncovered no crimes, only indiscretions. It added no new name to the list of City sharks, or to the shorter list of corrupt officials. It is best regarded now as a sociological study which will help in many a City case for centuries to come.

There was never the faintest possibility that the Lynskey affair would break the Attlee Government in Britain as the Daladier Government in France had been broken by the

RIGHT: Ferdinand de Lesseps

BELOW: Lesseps' project for the Suez Canal had run into financial difficulties but unlike the later Panama Canal project, Lesseps was able to finish it. Lesseps and friends in Alexandria, 1865

Stavisky affair in 1934. The latter also surfaced as a City case, but it is only the memory of a political crisis that survives.

Stavisky's was not the first City case in France involving a name internationally known. Notable among its predecessors was the Panama Scandal half a century before, a scandal for ever unhappily identified with the revered, colossal figure of Lesseps.

The entry under his name in a popular modern encyclopaedia repays scrutiny. 'Lesseps, Ferdinand, Vicomte de (1805–94); French diplomat and engineer; built Suez Canal, 1859–69; began Panama Canal, 1881.' Each fact correct, yet one is left with a false impression. Would you not infer – having regard to his life span – that he did not finish, as he 'began', the Panama Canal simply because of intervention by old age or death? Would you not infer – having regard to the dignity of 'diplomat' – that his career closed in an atmosphere of sanctity conferred by foreign embassies and the Quai d'Orsay? Probably. But both inferences would be wrong. The career of Lesseps closed in ignominy. He did not finish the Panama Canal because he was put out of business. His Panama Canal Company impoverished thousands, and expended millions to no useful end.

When a group of French entrepreneurs conceived the idea of piercing by canal the isthmus of Panama, it was natural that they should want Lesseps to be their leader. His unrivalled expertise and experience were ideal both for planning and for carrying out the work. His reputation, as a man of integrity as well as genius, was ideal for enlisting support and bringing in the cash. It was a misfortune for many besides Lesseps himself that, during his connection with the Panama Canal Company, neither his genius nor his integrity showed to much advantage.

The enterprise was obviously fraught with physical difficulties – but so had been Lesseps's earlier triumph at Suez. Now traffic flowed between the Red and Mediterranean Seas; why should it not flow – yielding a rich harvest of dues – between the Atlantic and Pacific Oceans? It is charitable to suppose that the great engineer's mental powers were failing, that he was bemused by dreams, not impelled by greed. But whatever the cause, his management of the project abounded in misrepresentation, negligence and waste.

69

As a sinister start, the public were deceived into subscribing. On the strength of a sketchy survey of the terrain by amateurs, Lesseps grossly underestimated costs (as he grossly over-estimated user tonnage). Worse, he backed his costings by a public statement that contractors of world-wide repute had agreed to do the job for twenty million pounds. That statement, in politest language, lacked foundation. No plant was forthwith rigged. Only the market was. A share issue went like wildfire, to set the company up with twelve million pounds.

This substantial sum was very quickly spent. Not in cutting, not in digging. The twelve million pounds poured forth in buying out, sometimes at an exorbitant price, concessionaires (for example the parallel Panama Railroad), not all of whom had been disclosed to the shareholders. Also, to a lesser but not trifling extent, in providing palatial homes and private railway cars for the staff of supervisors congregated on the site. More than once the company had to ask for further capital; more than once this was easily obtained. But as months and then years went by with nothing gathered in except an increasing crop of disturbing rumours, the mood in the Bourse (and in the cafes) changed. The Lesseps magic faded. Confidence disappeared. New issues were ignored – or positively vetoed. Ultimately the company ran clean out of funds, and the French scheme for a Panama Canal was revealed (I quote a crime historian of that day) as 'among the greatest financial fiascos of the world'.

The authorities, though understandably reluctant to move against a national idol in extreme old age, decided that to make an example was imperative. Lesseps – with others – was arraigned for fraud and sentenced to five years' imprisonment. The sentence was not enforced, but its mere pronouncement made a sad finale to an illustrious life. If Suez was written on Lesseps's monument, Panama must surely have been written on his heart.

The Canal itself, of course, has now been so long with us that our world is inconceivable without it. The United States, having acquired the necessary rights in 1902, organized and completed its construction. The first ship passed through in January 1914. Lesseps had then been dead for twenty years.

The Americans' bill amounted to more than three hundred and fifty million dollars.

America's principal contribution to the roll of City cases is appropriately modern and outsize and fantastic. As if the White House, Wall Street and the embryonic Pentagon had temporarily moved and been absorbed in Disneyland.

It perplexes me that the English – who avidly followed Watergate – have, for the most part, never so much as heard of Teapot Dome. Now and again, when journalists think that, nearer home, they scent collusion between Government and business, the words are dropped in the hope that they will be meaningful. 'Teapot Dome?' coyly enquired the headline of an article about some City (of London) transactions in the sixties. But that was in a 'quality' paper meant for 'intellectuals' (and I doubt if one in five of them understood the reference). Lack of knowledge leaves an empty space for misconceptions, so the most likely ones should forthwith be disposed of.

Teapot Dome did not concern, in any aspect, tea; there was no sale of plantations, no fiddling in tea shares. Nor was there a dome; no Xanadu, no Kubla Khan. Teapot Dome was the name of a tract of earth – earth which did not gush the sacred river Alph, but a more highly prized twentieth-century treasure: oil. That oil greased invisible skids beneath the President.

Warren Harding, who in 1921 succeeded Woodrow Wilson, died when he had been in office less than eighteen months. That, taking a long view, was his good fortune. Had he lived to complete his term, there would not have been on his demise what the *New York Times* described as 'the most remarkable demonstration in American history of affection, respect and reverence for the dead'. It is more likely that he would have been impeached.

Harding is America's forgotten President. Americans are willing, if not anxious, to forget him. His appearance, preserved in photographs, might make one wonder why. Superbly handsome, with a massive head and splendid bearing, he could well have exchanged his frock coat and top hat for a Roman toga and a laurel wreath. He looked the embodiment of patrician wisdom. He was, though, the embodiment of plebeian folly.

Mrs Harding pinpointed her husband's basic fault when, after their elevation, she announced that they were 'just

WARREN GAMALIEL HARDING
PRESIDENT OF THE UNITED STATES OF AMERICA
1920   1923

folks'. Just folks are not the stuff out of which real leaders are made; the opposite belief is democracy's delusion. Churchill, De Gaulle and Roosevelt were not just folks. They had extraordinary qualities for extraordinary tasks. Harding had not. He had risen above his mental and moral as well as social station.

For Harding was not only just folks; he was just folks from a small town. Marion, Ohio, where politics were conducted on back porches, with sing-songs, and at cards. As President (a perfect product of compromises in smoke-filled rooms), Harding gave key posts to his small-town cronies – not simply as rewards for helping put him where he was, but also because he wanted to have what Sinclair Lewis's Babbitt would have called 'the boys' around. At work as well as play. At the Cabinet, as well as at the poker, table. Such a predilection does not conduce to good appointments, and, even right outside the Marion circle, Harding (a poor picker) made some very bad ones. It is true that Hughes (at State) and Hoover (at Commerce) did him proud. But it is true that many, conversely, let him down. No one more badly than Albert B. Fall.

OPPOSITE: President Warren Harding.

LEFT: Albert B. Fall, Secretary of the Interior, 1922.

Fall's political background was as parochial as Harding's. His business connections, however, were at HQ level. He was 'in with' oil barons, and, when he was made Secretary of the Interior they considered him 'our man'. Not unjustifiably. Fall didn't jib at 'looking after' his old pals. Provided he got a little something in return.

Back in 1919, certain oil-bearing lands had been earmarked as reserves for the Navy's needs' One, in California, was Elks Hills. Another, in Wyoming, was Teapot Dome.

In 1920, Congress placed these lands in the custody of the Secretary of the Navy.

In March 1922, by Executive Order, President Harding transferred them into the custody of the Secretary of the Interior. Few noticed at the time, and those who did accepted it as an ordinary, run-of-the-mill, inter-departmental move.

In April 1922, Fall, secretly and without competitive bidding, leased the Teapot Dome Reserve to the Mammoth Company.

In December 1922, Fall, secretly and without competitive bidding, leased the Elks Hill reserve to the Pan-American Company.

Under each lease, the lessees were required to pay royalties. This could be – and has been – represented as an excellent arrangement for the Government. The royalties could buy fuel oil tanks, fill them and convey them to strategically sensitive locations. But there is little to sustain the proposition that this factor was uppermost in Secretary Fall's mind. Or that his primary objective was to benefit the nation. The data strongly indicates that his primary objective was to benefit his oil barons – and himself. For Fall received from the head of Mammoth $260,000 in Liberty Bonds. He received from the head of Pan-American $100,000 cash. The latter disbursement was explained, unconvincingly, as a loan. The former disbursement was not explained at all.

News of Teapot Dome – the leases had been so alike, in all respects, that the name of the earlier was used to cover both – only reached the public, via the Press, in 1924. The anger aroused initially was directed less at the criminals than at the detectives. Harding had been in his grave hardly a year, and many Democrats, as well as his own Republicans, felt that the disclosures verged on desecration. Not that the lid was wholely lifted in the early stages; it went on, inch by inch, till the end of the decade. There were Senate investigations. There were civil actions. There were criminal trials. There was long delay before the undercover handouts came to light. There was long delay before these were recognized as bribes. Then the leases were voided; then Fall was sentenced to a year's imprisonment; then a temperate chronicler could write, in 1931, that the Harding administration was responsible for more rascality than any other in the history of the Federal Government. (Chroniclers, of course, do not possess clairvoyance.)

It is impossible to believe that Fall was not acting deviously when he signed the leases. But is it impossible to believe that Harding was not acting deviously when he signed the Executive Order? Was the President a full participant in Teapot Dome? Or was he the innocent tool of his nefarious appointee?

I think the answer lies somewhere in between.

There is no concrete evidence – transcending frothy rumour – that Harding was an instigator or a beneficiary. One is compelled therefore, to rely on fallible pointers, such as presence or absence of motive and general character. Unlike Fall, Harding was not short of money, and never would be now. There were no children of the marriage for whom to pile up an inheritance. Teapot Dome? Gee, no; even if he'd been a villain – which, goshdarn, he wasn't – nothing to tempt Warren Harding in this Teapot Dome.

Nothing tangible, that is. No temptation to join in, and thus draw out. But might there be another, less obvious, temptation? A man liked to be popular, a man liked to be liked. Not least by 'the boys'. Most of all, by 'the boys'. So . . .

ABOVE: In October 1929 Fall was found guilty on charges of accepting bribes

75

RIGHT: A cartoon of 1929: the Teapot Dome Affair takes its place alongside the other great political scandals.

don't poke your nose in. Don't ask too many questions. If you wink an eye, that doesn't mean that you're a grafter. So wink an eye; wink an eye now and then. Better than have ole Albert get sore at ole Warren.

That is how I interpret the workings of Harding's mind – a mind more woolly than wicked, a mind less warped than weak. No other interpretation seems to me consistent with two unescapable truths about Teapot Dome. Harding was not active. Harding was aware.

At first, perhaps, not so aware as he had become in the summer of 1923 when he set out for Alaska. His behaviour on this visit was noticeably strange. Unwontedly nervous. Unaccountably apprehensive. Constantly seeking undefined reassurance. Plunging into unprecedented melancholy after reading messages, in code, from Washington. Whatever the degree of his antecedent privity, by then Harding surely knew what Fall had been up to.

Not even Harding's staunchest defenders can deny that, by using minimal diligence and foresight, he could at the very outset have killed Teapot Dome. Ironically enough, there have been speculations whether it was Teapot Dome that in

76

the end killed him. Indirectly, through ever-growing fear of disaster. The doctors named the cause of his death as apoplexy, following an attack of ptomaine poisoning. No one in the presidential entourage, sharing the presidential meals, got ptomaine poisoning. Some have suggested that he was poisoned deliberately by Mrs Harding, herself knowing all and resolved to save him from disgrace. Others have suggested that, for the same reason, he committed suicide. It strains credulity, though, that experienced doctors should be so deceived – or else accomplices in deception. Apoplexy gives rise to more feasible conjectures. A seizure, a stroke (as it is now more commonly called) may be occasioned, or at least accelerated, by the physical effects of psychological pressures. It may equally, of course, descend upon a happy man, at ease with his thoughts and at peace with his conscience. But it is hard to resist perceiving some correlation between President Harding's fatal stroke and the encroaching, thickening, shade of Teapot Dome.

The infamy of Harding is not truly parallel with that of his successor in our generation. Nixon was Tricky Dicky before he reached the Presidency. Harding was nothing worse than ole Warren. Nixon was clever to the point of being cunning. Harding was naïve to the point of being stupid. Nixon was ill-intentioned. Harding was ill-starred.

They do resemble one another, though, in this respect. Each bore a stupendous load of guilt, neither bore that stupendous load alone. And I do not allude to Mitchell or Haldeman or Fall. The British Prime Minister, Lord Melbourne, said last century: 'The people, as well as kings and ministers, are responsible to God for the exercise of power committed to their charge.' *The Dictionary of American Biography* paraphrases, amplifies and particularizes: 'A heavy responsibility for his [Harding's] record falls upon the party and nation which elected a man of moderate abilities, weak judgement of character, excessive amiability and total lack of vigilance.'

That, slightly cut, would serve as the speech in Harding's prosecution. It would also serve as the speech in his defence.

CHICAGO DAILY NEWS

COLDER

Tonight — Rain, ending, cloudy, windy, turning much colder, low in upper 20s. Saturday — Partly cloudy, much colder, high in the 30s.

Map and chart on Page 38.

FINAL MARKETS
RED STREAK

88TH YEAR—276   46 PAGES   FRIDAY, NOVEMBER 22, 1963   7 CENTS   ★   PHONE 321-2000

PRESIDENT IS KILLED

Texas Sniper Escapes; Johnson Sworn In

3.

POLITICAL MURDERS

Spencer Perceval
the attempt to murder
Lloyd George
John F. Kennedy
William McKinley
James A. Garfield
Abraham Lincoln
Rasputin
Mussolini
Mateotti

Murder of a politician is called assassination. The overtones of this substituted word are subtle. It does not suggest an act more venial, less shocking. It does suggest a less ignoble, more exalted motive. A murderer prompted by ideals or ideology commands respect, sometimes even sympathy, which is withheld from a murderer prompted by avarice or passion. A killing intended for public deliverance or vengeance does not incur moral opprobrium to the same degree as a killing intended for private satisfaction or advantage.

One British Prime Minister – so far, *only* one – has met his death by assassination. That he was victim of a grudge, not martyr to a cause, must rank high among the sourer pranks of fate.

The tale is told of a bishop, in past days, to whom someone sent a cryptic, unsigned, telegram. 'All is discovered; fly at once,' it said. The Most Reverend gentleman, if the tale may be believed, fled abroad that night and never reappeared. Such a tale could not credibly apply to Spencer Perceval.

PAGE 78: The final edition of the *Chicago Daily News*, 22 November 1963

RIGHT: Spencer Perceval, Prime Minister 1809–12

OPPOSITE: The assassination of Perceval in the lobby of the House of Commons, 11 May 1812: a contemporary print

Devoted husband, fond father, warm-hearted friend, his personal character was irreproachable. No trespasses to hide, no sins to expiate. He has claims to be considered the nicest of our premiers – as he is certainly among the most obscure. Gladstone and Disraeli, Pitt and Palmerston, even Peel and Canning, are still household names. But though Perceval, for three years, also held the highest office, he has been largely overshadowed and forgotten. His place in history is only guaranteed, not by his undramatic life, but by his dramatic death.

It occurred on 11 May 1812.

That afternoon, crossing the lobby of the House of Commons, Prime Minister Perceval, taken completely by surprise, was shot at close range straight through the heart with an ordinary pistol. By an ordinary person. One of those loiterers, one of those habitués, who attract no attention because they are so often there. Perceval had crumpled up and collapsed unconscious before the astonished onlookers could collect their wits. Not that, on a practical reckoning, it

mattered. The murderer made no attempt whatever to escape. A man of average height and unexceptional aspect, he sat down on a bench, laid his pistol at the side of him, and quietly waited. Before the shouts went up ('Shut the door! Let no one escape!'), he could have walked out and vanished, possibly for ever. But that would have defeated his calculated purpose. 'You need not press me,' he was to assure his captors. 'I submit myself to justice.' Few heard those words. Fewer, if they had done, would have understood them in the sense that they were intended to convey. Meanwhile, for lack of ascertainable motive, wild rumours amplified and spread.

The assassination of a head of Government is sometimes intrinsically hardly more appalling than the false inferences immediately drawn. Hundreds, or thousands, or millions think they recognize a sparking point of a vast conspiracy bent on undermining all existing institutions. The United States reacted thus to the slaying of John F. Kennedy; a century and a half before, with a statesman of less stature, England exhibited similar reactions. Perceval was liked as an individual, even by his strongest parliamentary opponents; but he governed at a period of widespread discontents, bitter grievances, festering resentments. The Napoleonic wars dragged on without success in sight, the cost and the blockade eroded the economy, poverty and hunger were giving rise to violence. Prime Ministers are nationally elected whipping boys, and obviously some would condemn Spencer Perceval for any and every privation or distress. But they were unlikely to condemn Perceval alone, or to suppose, if shedding blood seemed to them the remedy, that shedding his, by itself, would achieve their aim. Small wonder that most con-temporaries in high quarters followed (simultaneously for-tifying) precedent; that, with the French example so adjacent and so recent, they saw visions of the guillotine set up at Charing Cross and heard echoes of the tumbrils rattling down Whitehall. The uncertain temper of the mob that quickly filled the streets increased alarm and prompted drastic measures. The militia, the Foot Guards, and the Horse Guards were called out 'to preserve the peace of the Met-ropolis'. But apprehensions of a general upheaval were dispelled by a calm and voluntary statement from the killer.

LEFT: John Bellingham in the dock at the Old Bailey, 15 May 1812; a contemporary engraving

His name was John Bellingham. He was not a revolutionary; he had neither taste nor time for revolutions. He was not the sparking point of a conspiracy; he had neither accomplices nor backers. He was not discontented with, or resentful of, wartime hardships and austerities; he had been too pre-occupied to notice them. But he did nourish a very bitter grievance, one peculiarly and exclusively his own. In 1804, at the age of thirty-three, he had gone out as a merchant's agent to Archangel, meaning to stay no more than a few months. He got involved, however, in a business dispute which led to the cancellation of his exit pass, and, for the next five years, was detained in Russia; under strict surveillance when not actually imprisoned. Bellingham blamed two governments for his ordeal: the Russian, which he charged with persecution and injustice; the British, which he charged with neglect and lack of zeal in striving for his release through its representatives. The first charge seems not totally unwarranted, the second dubious and debatable. But there is no doubt, at any rate, of this – that Bellingham returned to his native land resolved to exact compensation and obtain redress for what he deemed gross and grievous dereliction of Britain's duty to a British citizen.

He threw himself into the task with concentration. His attention to his wife and children, so long parted from him, was affectionate but abstracted. His attention to his ship-broking affairs, so long suspended, was imperative but perfunctory. His thoughts, and frequently his actions, were elsewhere. Tirelessly, persistently, he composed memorials and handed in petitions to the Home Office, the Foreign Office, the Treasury Commissioners, the Prince Regent, the Bow Street magistrates. One supplication was dispatched to Spencer Perceval; a secretary dispatched a negative reply. When, two years later, another supplication to another personage reaped as its sole fruit the maddening advice that the complaint should be addressed to Mr Perceval, Bellingham abandoned faith in polite procedures. He concluded that the only way to gain publicity, and the judgement in his favour he felt sure must follow, was to kill the forty-nine-year-old Prime Minister. He harboured no spite against Perceval as Perceval. He stressed afterwards that he shot the Minister, not the man. There may have been an element of reprisal in the shooting ('I'll do unto you as they did unto me'); but, if so, it was slight and almost incidental. What he wanted was a forum where he could present his case. That was why he said 'I submit myself to justice.'

The crime was planned with a methodical thoroughness which would have been admirable in a worthier enterprise. On 20 April, three weeks before the murder, Bellingham bought a brace of pistols, each *seven* inches long. He made himself familiar with the working of these pistols by informal target practises on Primrose Hill. He instructed a tailor to cut a pocket, *nine* inches deep, on the inside of his coat. He haunted the gallery of the House of Commons, inquiring from his neighbours which minister was which, and examined through an opera glass those identified. His eyes returned repeatedly to Spencer Perceval. The evidence of pre-meditation verged on surplusage.

84

It was right that retribution should not have been slow, but wrong that it should have been nearly instantaneous. The barest outline of the timetable speaks volumes. Monday, at 5.15 pm, the murder. Friday, the trial, the verdict and the sentence. Monday next, at 8.00 am, the execution. Less than a complete week from guilt to gallows. The law, often criticized for gross delays, here may be criticized for unseemly haste. The fact that there can be no real defence to an indictment should not bar the accused from opportunity to prepare one.

No real defence? What about insanity? Mollie Gillen, who wrote *Assassination of the Prime Minister*, has studied Bellingham as carefully as anyone alive. She asserts that he was 'a man clearly insane'. I venture to dissent from that opinion. Though Bellingham himself claimed that his act was justified, defending counsel – I suspect in desperation – did raise the question of his client's mental state. It became, inevitably, the one substantial issue. The M'Naghten Rules (examined on another page) were not enunciated till a later generation. But Lord Chief Justice Mansfield's summing-up anticipated them. Had the prisoner possessed, he asked, sufficient understanding to distinguish good from evil, right from wrong? The jury answered yes. I think we may do, also.

Bellingham was far from being 'clearly insane'. He had an *idée fixe*. So had many others. That does not free them from responsibility for what they do. Bellingham was no more mad than Neill Cream. No more mad than Christie. No more mad than Haigh.

The British Prime Minister least like Spencer Perceval is Lloyd George. A great man, but not a nice man. A magnetic personality, but not a flawless character. A parliamentarian and a demagogue of genius, but an unchivalrous adversary and untrustworthy friend. Mentally outstanding, sexually promiscuous; politically masterful, financially corrupt; extravagantly idolized, venomously hated; a giant in his own age, in history an immortal. Everything Perceval wasn't, nothing Perceval was. The sole respect in which they correspond is that each led the nation during a crucial clash of arms. Even that resemblance, though, is neutralized by a disparity. Perceval died while the battle raged and the

outcome lay in doubt. Lloyd George lived to make the peace as The Man Who Won The War.

It might have been otherwise, if, in 1917, the Secret Service had not unearthed a plot to murder him.

The driving force in this plot was Mrs Wheeldon, a widow with a second-hand clothes business in Derby. She and her grown-up children were known locally as 'cranks'; they held and ventilated unpopular views on various disputed questions of the day. They were all what have aptly been called 'belligerent pacifists'; one son was a conscientious objector, two daughters (like their mother) were militant suffragettes. Apparently they needed to personalize their feelings, and their pacifism specially found expression and release in an obsessive animosity against Lloyd George. This presently assumed a form more dangerous than fostering ugly thoughts and uttering angry words. Mrs Wheeldon procured from her son-in-law, a chemical operative, sufficient strychnine to poison fifteen people, and actively sought means of administering a lethal dose to their *bête noir*.

What benefit did they suppose would attend success? Impossible to state, hard even to surmise. They were not German agents, Sinn Feiners, Communists. They had nothing to gain from Lloyd George's liquidation. F. E. Smith,

OPPOSITE: Lloyd George and his family in 1917

BELOW: F. E. Smith who, as Attorney-General, prosecuted the Wheeldons

who, as Attorney-General, prosecuted them, wondered whether they had ever looked ahead at all. 'It may be,' he wrote (some years later, as Lord Birkenhead), 'that his death was all they wanted. *Finis coronat opus.*' Whether or no, the Wheeldons had no personal axe to grind. Theirs would have been a true political murder – a case of a man being murdered for his politics.

Even an abortive conspiracy to murder that particular politician at that particular time created a sensation which has had no parallel. The trial was treated like war news – as in a way it was. The sentences (ten years for the ringleader, seven for her son-in-law, five for his wife) were acclaimed like victories – as in a way they were. The Wheeldons touched a peak of notoriety, then vanished; subsequent annalists have generally ignored them. They have been consigned to the historian's limbo – perhaps through instinctive repugnance and distaste. For in post-Perceval England, what they set out to do simply isn't done.

It is done, with sickening regularity, abroad. Even among folk whom we consider kith and kin. Occupational risk is greater at the White House than at Downing Street. Of America's thirty-seven presidents (the same total, roughly, as that of our Prime Ministers), no fewer than four have been murdered while in office, a proportion high enough to worry actuaries. There is no obvious explanation for this figure. The murders were not variations on a constant theme. Only one of the murderers was clearly motivated by a factional or political belief. Two were motivated – more or less like Bellingham – by individual circumstance and crotchet. And the motive behind the most recent of these murders has still not been satisfactorily solved.

The official version is that John F. Kennedy was murdered, at Dallas in 1963, by Lee Harvey Oswald, and by him alone. The putative murderer was himself summarily murdered, and none of the motives since ascribed to him seem rational if plausible, plausible if rational. The official version, then, would make a controversial President a victim of a creature either mindless or deranged. That may well be so. The Warren Commission of investigation, set up by Lyndon Johnson, Kennedy's successor, pointed strongly and solely

towards Oswald, but stressed the difficulty of proving negatives (that is, that no other person was involved). So, as Theodore C. Sorensen writes in his book *Kennedy*, 'We can never be absolutely certain whether some other hand might not have *coached, coaxed, or coerced* . . . Kennedy's killer.' In the context of Big D, a city symbolizing almost everything the murdered President was against, one is not left at a loss for speculation on those lines. I acquiesce in, rather than support, the official version. It is the likeliest, on the evidence produced. An element of mystery, though, markedly persists.

No mystery whatever attaches to the shooting of Kennedy's three presidential predecessors.

William McKinley had been elected in 1896, and, proving one of the electorate's wiser choices, was voted back in 1900 for a second term. In September 1901 he visited Buffalo to attend the Pan-American Exposition. He delivered a major policy speech there on the 5th; on the 6th he was fatally wounded by a bullet as members of the public queued to shake his hand. His assailant, twenty-eight years old, son of Polish immigrants, was a professed anarchist unencumbered with ideas – save that anyone in any authority should die. He pored over accounts and pictures of assassinations like some men pore over girlie magazines. Leon Czolgosz did not shoot McKinley because of the doctrines the latter preached or causes he upheld; those would have been beyond his knowledge and his grasp. He shot him simply because he held a post of power. The twenty-fourth President of the United States was murdered by an impersonal fanatic. Now he might have gone to hospital as a so-called psychopath. Then as a cold-blooded killer he went to the chair.

James A. Garfield had been elected in 1880, a compromise candidate of the Republicans, nominated after thirty-six convention ballots. In July 1881, boarding a train to leave the capital, he was fatally wounded – like McKinley – by a bullet, though he lingered on painfully for many weeks. His assailant, Charles Guiteau, thirty-nine years old, was a hack writer, a fervent evangelist and a professional crook. He had given McKinley valueless support at the election and expected a patronage job as his reward. When, despite badgering demands, he didn't get it, he volunteered unwanted services to rebellious senators and, a month before the crime, purchased a revolver. He pretended at first that he had acted altruistically to save the Republican Party from a destructive chief, but soon abandoned that unconvincing hocus-pocus. At trial he had the shrewdness to plead insanity. The jury had the shrewdness to disregard that plea. The twentieth President of the United States was murdered by a disappointed place-seeker. Guiteau, however, was not electrocuted. He was hanged.

The sixteenth President also died by an assassin's bullet. Like the twentieth. Like the twenty-fourth. But neither they nor any other President – not even Franklin Roosevelt, not even George Washington – may be mentioned, without blasphemy, in the same breath as he. For the sixteenth President has been almost deified. At very least he ranks with Shakespeare and Napoleon among mortals in the splendour of his glory and the fullness of his fame.

That, however, is a posthumous assessment. His contemporaries, foe and friend alike, would be astonished if they could see the halo nowadays encircling Abraham Lincoln's rugged head.

He was born in 1809 in the proverbial log cabin on a barren farm in the backwoods of Kentucky. He moved westwards by stages to Springfield, Illinois, an expanding village which became his home. Till he reached forty-five, an age when most men have revealed their maximum potential, he remained a small town lawyer and provincial politician, neither tipped for, nor aspiring to, national prominence. He invoked trust by his manifest integrity, he stirred emotions by his simple eloquence, but, even after broadening his scope in middle life, he was not thought to possess that majesty of mind which befits a leader and denotes a statesman. His choice as Republican presidential candidate, in 1860, came as a surprise; his election, as the Southern states prepared to secede, owed much to a split among the Democrats; his conduct of affairs in the subsequent four years of strife excited widespread and diverse criticism; his nomination for a second term met serious resistance; his re-election, when at last victory in the field was sure, hung in the balance almost up to the last moment. And finally, his assassination – five days after Lee had surrendered at Appomattox – created instant shock rather than enduring grief. Many admired him,

many liked him, many followed him, but no one held Lincoln in reverence and awe.

To an age when everyone holds him in reverence and awe, this unembellished record may seem barely credible. Lincoln cannot have changed. Why, then, should his image? The explanation rests in a myth, which has ousted history, about the nature of the Civil War.

The myth is that the war occurred entirely over slavery; that the North (the good guys) wanted to abolish it; that the South (the bad guys) wanted to retain it; that battle was joined on a moral principle, and that Lincoln led the side that morally was right. A picture marred by omissions and distortions, rendered more misleading because certain parts are true.

It is true that the Southern states countenanced slavery. It is true that the Northern states did not. It is true that Lincoln himself detested it. 'If slavery is not wrong, nothing is wrong,' he said. But slavery, aye or nay, was a secondary matter. Lincoln would not – could not – have led the North into a war merely to eradicate slavery in the South. Lincoln did lead the North into a war to defend the effective existence of the Union. Any other crusade which he might espouse was incidental to this overriding aim. 'If I could save the Union,' he said, 'by emancipating all the slaves, I would do so; if I could save it by emancipating none of them, I would do so; if I could save it by emancipating some and not others, I would do that too.' And as he did not believe the Union could long survive 'half slave and half free', he proclaimed emancipation in the middle of the war, ensuring total abolition if the North should win. But slavery was still a secondary matter. The principle at stake was political, not moral. Federal Union or loose Confederacy? Central government or individual state autonomy? That was the main issue of the war in which Lincoln led the side which ultimately triumphed.

Who were the freedom fighters in this fratricidal conflict? The Northerners thought they were – they fought for human rights. The Southerners thought they were – they fought for independence. Foreign, including British, sympathy lay, at the beginning, with the South. But, since the dust has settled, Southerners themselves, excepting a diehard, dwindling, minority, acknowledge that events have justified the North.

LEFT: Abraham Lincoln, 1864

93

Understand that, and much beside can be understood. The estimate of Lincoln changing down the years. The superficial paradox of his assassination. The words that his assassin uttered as he struck.

Ford's Theatre was packed that night, not simply for the play. News had got round Washington that a bigger, rarer, attraction would be offered. The President, his laurels fresh upon him, had decided to enjoy a little relaxation.

As the ungainly figure – Lincoln was six foot four and disproportionately lean – shambled behind his wife into their box, the audience gave him a spontaneous ovation. One person present, though, did not join in. He lurked in the shadows, taut and tense, masking his impatience.

BELOW LEFT: The playbill for Ford's Theatre, 14 April 1865, the night Lincoln was assassinated there

BELOW RIGHT: John Wilkes Booth

John Wilkes Booth belonged to a great theatrical family; not unlike the Terrys, not unlike the Barrymores. Less famous than his father and his brother (who was playing Hamlet in Boston on that very night), he had nonetheless acquired some reputation as a romantic, athletic juvenile, specializing in the type of role since associated with the elder Douglas Fairbanks. He was well known to employees at Ford's Theatre, and would be free to come and go almost as he pleased. Moreover, he knew the theatre's geography – an important asset in carrying out his plans.

Not that his plans had anything to do with his profession. The war and its outcome had driven all else from his mind. A Southern zealot, rabid and embittered, he was head and mainspring of an underground conspiracy to murder members of the Federal Government. The Vice-President and Secretary of State had been allotted to accomplices. Booth had reserved the principal offender for himself.

BELOW: The assassination of Abraham Lincoln, after a painting by Joseph Beale

ABOVE: The death of
Lincoln

The performance was in full swing when he crept stealthily
along the small corridor which led to Lincoln's box. He
paused, and, safe from observation, drew a gun. Noiselessly,
inch by inch, he opened the box door. Inside, the solitary
attendant never turned. Absorbed by the farce being enacted
down below, he was ignorant of the tragedy impending from
behind. The back of Lincoln's head, an unprotected target,
presented itself only a yard or two away. Booth fired one shot.
It was enough. As the President fell forward, as wild uproar
arose, he jumped over the ledge of the box twelve feet on to
the stage. '*Sic semper tyrannis,*' he cried. Then, gun still in
hand, he dashed out through the rear, leaped on to a waiting
horse and galloped off, exulting. Lincoln was a fortnight dead
when Booth, brought to bay in Maryland, was himself shot
dead, resisting to the last, trapped in a barn set ablaze by his
pursuers.

Sic semper tyrannis was the motto of Virginia, but it also
expressed Booth's inward feelings at that moment. Lincoln
himself once said on the subject of assassinations: 'An
enthusiast broods over the oppression of a people till he
fancies himself commissioned by Heaven to liberate them.'
Replace 'liberate' by 'avenge', and those words apply to
Booth. To us, he was a wicked man who slew a liberator. To
himself, he was a liberator who slew a wicked man.

Of course Booth's judgement was warped and ludicrous. Lincoln, if not a god, was among the best of men. As Rasputin, if not the devil incarnate, was among the worst.

The mind's eye conjures up at once a portrait of Rasputin. Thick hair. Thicker beard. Large nose. Piercing eye. Gross lips. Enormous bulk. An aura of the dark and sinister. But that portrait barely hints at the repulsiveness of the original. Hair matted. Beard tangled. Nose fleshy. Eye lustful. Lip pendulous. Bulk filthy. An aura of iniquity and corruption. And even that front barely hints at the depravity within. Parading a monk's garb and a monk's pretentions, Rasputin seduced simple women, debauched innocent girls, and eagerly participated in Bacchanalian orgies which would have caused remark at the court of Elagabalus. A drunkard, a libertine, a hypocrite . . . a monster.

There have been other monsters in quasi-human form. Some notable only for their monstrosities: Jack the Ripper, Peter Kurten, Irma Grese. Some notable apart from their monstrosities: Herod, Henry VIII, Benito Mussolini. But these latter had advantages of ability or birth. How did it come about that a Siberian peasant, almost illiterate as well as wholly vicious, with no mental capacity higher than low cunning, was the virtual ruler of the old Russian Empire for several years before its extinction during the First World War?

The key rests with the royal house of Romanov in the persons of the Tsar, the Tsaritsa, the Tsarevitch, destined each to be the last of their kind and line.

Imperial Russia was an autocracy and the Tsar an absolute monarch. But Nicholas II, who acceded in 1894 at the age of twenty-six, was weak, gentle – and uxorious; he had the authority to govern, but he lacked the will. The Tsaritsa was wilful, strong – and interfering; to all intents and purposes, she governed in his stead. The Tsarevitch, their son and heir, the dynasty's hope, his mother's idol, had been from birth afflicted with haemophilia. He bled profusely at the slightest hurt, and doctors could neither check the flow nor mitigate the pain. The disease, they said, is certain to prove fatal; the patient had done well to survive infancy, they said; attacks, they said, were bound to recur and the danger bound to grow. The most severe and dangerous attack thus far developed when the Tsarevitch was between three and four. The doctors shook their heads, the parents wrung their hands, the little boy's remaining hours upon this earth seemed numbered – till Rasputin dramatically appeared upon the scene.

That he should have been conveniently waiting in the wings was the chance that launched his meteoric rise. Professionally a 'holy man' – and nothing else besides – he had made, from early manhood, pilgrimages on foot which took him from his village home for months or even years. He was thirty on his first pilgrimage to the capital, St Petersburg (later Petrograd, later Leningrad). He kept returning and finally stayed for good, only paying visits at decreasing intervals to his docile wife and children still beyond the Urals.

RIGHT: Grigoire Rasputin

In St Petersburg, Rasputin won some cheap fame as a healer, reputedly receiving inspiration from above. This brought him to the notice of a gullible Grand Duchess who brought him to the notice of a gullible Tsaritsa. When the Tsarevitch was apparently *in extremis*, the Tsaritsa remembered and summoned the holy man. Rasputin entered the nursery, approached the bed, prayed over the child, told him not to be afraid, promised his pains would go. They did – within the hour. Next day he woke bright and cheerful. Next week, he was well. The doctors were astounded – and confounded; the Tsaritsa (and the Tsar) were overwhelmed with joy. It bore all the indications of a miracle.

As there were repetitions of this strange coincidence, it marked a turning point for the unfortunate Tsarevitch. It marked a bigger one for the fortunate Rasputin. Believing her son's life depended on his ministrations, the Tsaritsa henceforth tried to keep him within call. Convinced he was omnipotent, she inferred he was omniscient; she asked, and accepted, his advice on many matters – political, diplomatic, even military – which the holy man knew nothing about at all. Great events, however, might hinge on his lightest word. The Tsar had always been under the Tsaritsa's thumb. The Tsaritsa now was under Rasputin's. The mightiest, if he so decided, could lose rank or favour; no one felt safe from his malice and his mischief. Not a bishop. Not a general. Not a minister.

With the onset of war and the approach of revolution, private and patriotic feelings merged. The threat to individuals was perceived, more plainly, as a threat to the nation as a whole. Except for a capricious clique of well-born ladies, perversely smitten by this fetid charlatan, high society sank its differences and united in resolve to get rid of Rasputin. As the Tsaritsa's faith in her guru was as unshakable as the Tsar's subjection to his spouse, and Rasputin, prizing power more than gold, was proof against the largest cash temptation into exile, only one procedure remained. Assassination. At least nine plots had failed before the hour produced the man. Prince Felix Youssupov.

The Prince lived to tell the tale – twice told it publicly; each time without equivocation. Once in a book, *La Fin de Raspoutine*, published in Paris ten years after the event. Once,

years later still, in London, in the box, as a witness in his
wife's suit for defamation against Metro-Goldwyn-Mayer
arising from their film *Rasputin, the Mad Monk.* The libel?
That Rasputin had slept with her or raped her. The damages?
£25,000. Youssupov's story did not vary from one version to
another, withstood the test of rigorous cross-examination,
and I rely and draw upon it here.

His family was the oldest and wealthiest in Russia. Prince
Felix himself had been at Oxford, and had married a niece of
the Tsar. A young man of aesthetic bent and sensibility, he
contemplated any act of violence with disgust. But he was also
a young man of honour, not least where the interests of his
country were concerned. By December 1916 he had satisfied
himself that those interests demanded the removal of Rasputin. And as others who thought likewise had so often tried
in vain, he deemed it his solemn duty to accomplish murder.
The mixture of mission and repugnance with which he faced
this task puts him in the company of Charlotte Corday.

As a first step towards his object, he made acquaintance
with and affected a liking for Rasputin, sorely though that
must have gone against the grain. As a second step, he
brought into conspiracy four trusted intimates, one a doctor
who undertook to procure and handle cyanide. As a third
step, he invited Rasputin to visit him socially at the Moika
Palace – one of three the Youssupovs possessed in Petrograd.

On the evening the Prince appointed for the visit, he knew that his parents and his wife would be away.

Rasputin had agreed to come, but as a precaution his host called and fetched him from his home. At the palace, Youssupov led him to a basement room, one which, while safe from intrusion by the servants, was furnished in a style that would obviate suspicion. Cakes and wine were set out on a table; each cake, each glass, containing a dose of poison much more than enough to kill a man at once.

It was a grotesque *tête-à-tête* between prince and peasant. Youssupov pressing refreshment on Rasputin, Rasputin vexingly slow in his response. Eat, my friend, eat – they have been specially prepared. Join me, then. Of course – but, as a guest, it is your privilege. Yielding to aristocratic insistence upon etiquette, Rasputin swallowed a cake, swallowed another, smacked his lips. Nothing happened. They are good, my friend? Excellent. A drink to wash them down? Rasputin drank two glassfuls. Still nothing happened. Youssupov stared aghast. Was the creature immune to cyanide? Was he not of mortal flesh? That should forthwith be tested. Youssupov fired a pistol, aiming carefully at the heart. Rasputin fell, a red stain spreading across his blouse. The other conspirators, waiting above, heard the shot and hurried down. All, including the doctor, pronounced Rasputin dead.

But as they discussed their next move, the disposal of the corpse, it rose and leapt, clawing, at the Prince's throat. Youssupov struggled free. Rasputin somehow crawled up the cellar stairs and out to the courtyard. There bullets and blows and kicks rained on his giant frame – which police retrieved, several days later, from the river. An autopsy revealed that his lungs were full of water. Significant evidence. When the conspirators threw him in, Rasputin had been *still* alive.

His name and appearance have proved just as durable. They are familiar to the most uneducated and remote. During the last war, a well-known West End character was a constable who, in that shaven age, sported a full black beard. Off duty once, at my local pub, he got into conversation with a couple of GIs, Middle West farm boys who would have gaped uncomprehendingly if you had mentioned Coolidge. When they left, the constable said 'So long, Yanks.' 'So long,' one of them replied. 'So long, Rasputin.'

Mussolini played some part in at least three assassinations. Concluding – poetic justice – with his own.

That occurred on 28 April 1945, less than a week before VE Day in the last world war.

The Germans were pulling out of Italy. Dozens of convoys headed for the northern frontier, hoping somehow to reach the fatherland. The countryside teemed with Partisans of the Italian underground who hated the Germans, hated Italy's alliance with them, hated, most of all, Mussolini and his Fascists who had dragged Italy into that alliance. They rejoiced to see the Germans go, but wanted to make sure that no collaborating Italians escaped with them. So, whenever possible, they halted and inspected the retreating convoys. Notably one at Menaggio, on Lake Como.

The Partisans pulled from a lorry someone almost hidden by a heap of petrol cans; someone wearing a German army greatcoat, collar pulled over the mouth, and a matching helmet, tipped over the face. Pull the collar down, the helmet off, and there was not a doubt. That jutting jaw, those bulging eyes. They had got the biggest prize. They had caught *Il Duce*.

They telephoned the news to headquarters at Milan. Hold him; a senior commander will be dispatched at once. Meanwhile, in the village house where he was held, Mussolini asked his guards to carry his fond greetings to a woman, taken from another vehicle in the convoy, also detained, on suspicion, at a house near by.

'Who is she?' asked the guard. 'Don't hesitate to tell us. We can check up on her soon enough. Who is she?'

Mussolini whispered.

'Signora Petacci.'

'*The* Petacci?'

'*The* Petacci. You know of her then?'

Of course the guard knew of her. Everybody knew of her. Claretta Petacci was Mussolini's mistress. In recent years she had had great influence upon him, and as recent years had brought disaster on disaster, few Italians entertained friendly feelings for her. But one tribute must be paid to the Petacci: she was loyal. Any time in those last few weeks she could have cut adrift, gaining obscurity and safety for herself. But she chose differently, following Mussolini's path wherever it

102

might lead. She really loved that cardboard Bonaparte, and made only one request when she received his message.

'Take me to him. Lock me up in the same room. I want to share his fate. If you kill him, kill me too.'

Even the hardbitten Como Partisans could not close their hearts to such devotion, and the commander from headquarters found the pair together.

He addressed them with stern formality.

'Benito Mussolini. Claretta Petacci. We must leave here at once.'

'Who are you?' asked Mussolini. 'And what do you want with us?'

'I am Colonel Valerio. I have come to . . . set you free.'

Mussolini grasped at a straw which was not there, and offered a reward which was not his to bestow.

'If that is so, I give you the Empire,' he replied.

Valerio, however, had not come to bargain or to banter. He had come to carry out inexorable orders. With Mussolini and Claretta in the back of his car and a Partisan beside him, giving him directions, he drove to a deserted road where there was a high, blank, wall.

'All right,' Valerio said. 'Get out, Mussolini.'

'What does this mean?'

'You'll see. Get out and walk towards the wall.'

'I, too, then,' said Claretta.

Valerio shrugged.

'As you please.'

They got out. The *Duce* and his woman; the gangster and his moll. They turned at the same moment – to face the rifles, pointing.

'But Colonel,' Mussolini pleaded, 'What have I done to you?'

Claretta shrieked.

'No! No! He must not die!'

The rifles cracked. Deliberately she threw herself between them and their target.

'She asked for it,' said Valerio. 'Go and see.'

The Partisan strolled over. Prodded the recumbent man and woman with his foot.

'Yes. Dead. Both.'

'Stand by, then.' Valerio surveyed the tableau cynically.

'*They* were shown mercy. It did not take *them* long to die.'

The guard stood by the bodies, not to do them honour, but to ensure that they were not removed. Headquarters planned for Mussolini, who had so often postured and ranted upon balconies, a final public performance, a last farewell to the crowd.

It was evening when Valerio returned – this time, not with a car, but with an open truck. In the village yonder, they had been rounding up other Fascists, and the truck was loaded, higgledy piggledy, with corpses. Mussolini and Claretta were tossed on to the rest. Valerio waved dismissal to the guard, and drove off westward into the gathering night.

Early next day a hideous sound spread through Milan. A mixture of anger, loathing, triumph and lewd hilarity. This swelled to a crescendo, sustained hour after hour. But in the Piazzale Loreto, where it originated, the hideous sound was secondary to the hideous sight.

BELOW: The bodies of Mussolini and the Petacci hang between those of other leading Fascists

Mussolini and the Petacci, close together, hung by their heels from meat hooks. On either side, as if dancing attendance, former Fascist dignitaries similarly dangled. But the *Duce* and his consort were the magnet for the mob; it was on them that they visited their long pent-up emotions. They not merely booed and hissed, not merely reviled and jeered, not merely spat and threw filth at the swinging bodies. They treated those empty shells as if they still held life. Stabbing, slashing, kicking, even shooting, and, as one outrage followed on another, baying and howling and bellowing delight. Killing their enemies after they were dead, imagining that they themselves were actually doing the job already done by Colonel Valerio on their behalf.

Valerio – a Partisan *nom de guerre* – never concealed or tried to minimize his role. He wrote and spoke about it freely, and with pride. Understandable pride, so far as Mussolini was concerned, for even if one has a British lawyer's bias towards strict trial and orderly procedure, it is difficult to reprobate an action which rid the world of such a prodigious villain. But, in the very different case of the Petacci, one does not need a lawyer's vocational bias to regret that Valerio was quite so quick on the draw. As Churchill minuted Field-Marshal Alexander: 'Was *she* on the list of war criminals?'

RIGHT: Austria's 'Little Chancellor'; Dollfuss was assassinated by the Nazis in 1934

ABOVE: Dollfuss lies in state in Vienna

The word 'connive' is increasingly used as a synonym for 'conspire'. A confusing and wasteful error in semantics. Mussolini may have connived at (that is, closed his eyes to) the assassination of Dollfuss in 1934. He certainly conspired (that is, combined with others) to assassinate Matteotti in 1924.

It has sometimes been called the Matteotti mystery. A neo-Fascist euphemism hopefully covering up the fact that Mussolini was a common murderer. Actually, Matteotti's death is now no more mysterious than that of Thomas à Becket.

Matteotti was an Italian Socialist deputy. The deputy
hated the *Duce* as a despot; the Socialist hated him as a
renegade; the Italian hated him as a counterfeit Mazzini.
Mussolini returned this hatred in good measure. He also,
with cause, feared Matteotti as a popular rallying point of
discontent with the regime.

On 30 May 1924, in the Chamber, Matteotti denounced
Fascist violence during the previous elections. He moved that
they be declared void and for a new poll. His speech was
received by the Fascist majority with insults and threats, and,
as he sat down, he said to colleagues round him: 'Now you can
get ready for my funeral.'

On 10 June, walking in daylight through the streets of
Rome, Matteotti was dragged into a car, beaten up, and
stabbed. His body, nude and headless, was found trampled
into a ditch – two months later, forty miles away.

Meanwhile (on 12 June), as the whole country buzzed with
rumour, questions were asked of Mussolini as Prime Minister. Matteotti, he said in the Chamber, 'has unexpectedly
disappeared in circumstances of time and place not yet
definite, but which can support the hypothesis of a crime that,
if it has been committed, can only arouse the indignation and
grief of Parliament.' Characteristically, Mussolini tried to be
clever; just as characteristically, he gave away too much. A
Socialist deputy voiced the apprehension felt by millions.
'Then Matteotti is dead,' he cried. 'Let the Prime Minister

LEFT: A contemporary caricature of Mussolini implying his complicity in the murder of Matteotti was published in the clandestine Italian newspaper *Becco Giallo*

speak,' cried another deputy – less an appeal for a hearing than a demand for an explanation. Mussolini, however, ventured not a word. 'Then he is an accomplice,' the same deputy exclaimed. The enraged Fascists would have torn him limb from limb, but the intrepid deputy had not exaggerated.

Although never brought to the Bar in a court of justice, Mussolini stands convicted at the Bar of history. Motive? That must already be apparent. Opportunity? A dictator, within his frontiers, never lacks it. (Who decreed that Matteotti's usual police guardian should refrain from tailing him on that particular day?) Those, though, are only launching platforms. What beyond?

The vital clue was the index number of the kidnap car – jotted down by a quick-witted bystander. That led to the car's proprietor, one Filipelli, editor of a Fascist journal and Mussolini's friend. That led to the man who was lent the car specifically for the kidnap, one Dumini, on the staff of Mussolini's Press bureau, and also the boss of a small strong-arm group. Filipelli admitted that Mussolini personally had given the order for Matteotti's murder.

Indeed, Mussolini made a qualified confession in the Chamber on 3 January 1925. 'I alone,' he said, 'assume the moral responsibility for everything that has happened.' Ostensibly he spoke about the whole grim catalogue of Fascist crimes till then. But the context of the speech makes it crystal clear that in the forefront of his mind was Matteotti.

Morally responsible? As Lady Macbeth was morally responsible for the death of Duncan. As Brutus was morally responsible for the death of Caesar.

Dear Sir!

Have 50.000 $ ready, 25.000 $ in
20 $ bills 15000 $ in 10 $ bills and
10.000 $ in 5 $ bills. After 2-4 days
we will inform you will be deliver
the money.

We warn you for making
anyding public or for notify the police
the child is in gute care.

Indication for all letters are
singnature

and 3 holds.

4.

KIDNAPPING

**Elizabeth Canning
the Lindbergh baby
James Cross
Pierre Laporte
Samuel Bronfman
Muriel McKay
hi-jacking**

Each generation in turn believes it has invented sex. With rather more reason, ours believes it has invented kidnapping. We have at least converted a cottage industry into mass production. KIDNAP LATEST: DIPLOMAT HELD BY TERRORISTS: PEER'S HEIR SNATCHED IN STREET: RANSOM NOTE FOUND: HOSTAGE MURDER THREAT – the posters and headlines constantly signal the repetitive news, until today's crime is confused with yesterday's and supplanted by tomorrow's. Making full allowance for greater speed and coverage by the media, there certainly seem to be far more kidnappings now than ever before. But is the difference one of numbers only? Or is there also a difference of kind?

Nihil sub sole novum, says the Vulgate. And that goes even for Miss Patty Hearst. Was she *really* taken away against her will, or was her 'kidnapping', it has been asked, a cover for something she wanted to do anyway – join the Symbionese Liberation Army? After all that has since transpired and been flashed across the world, we still cannot be quite sure, and never will be. There are those, for whom history begins after VE Day and criminal history with Ruth Ellis or Hanratty, who think this Californian enigma wholly novel, a kidnap case

PAGE 110: The ransom note left on the window sill of the Lindbergh nursery

RIGHT: Patty Hearst and her fiancé, Stephen Weed, shortly before the kidnapping

ABOVE LEFT: The photograph issued by the Symbionese Liberation Army accompanying a tape which claimed that the heiress had become a member of their movement and had taken the name of Tania

ABOVE RIGHT: The massive food handout paid for by Randolph Hearst as part of the ransom demanded by the kidnappers of his daughter

LEFT: Patty Hearst photographed by a hidden camera during a bank robbery staged by members of the Symbionese Liberation Army

with an unprecedented twist. And yet one may fairly bracket with it another, which occurred in London more than two centuries ago. And, not unlike Patty Hearst, the central figure – a girl roughly the same age – was for about a year, according to Edmund Pearson, 'probably the most famous person in the world'.

The similarities of her adventure with that of Patty Hearst are set off by the contrasts in their personalities. Elizabeth Canning's family was of humble station. She herself was a tradesman's household serving-maid. She was disciplined, docile, in every way respectable, without either subversive ideas or disreputable friends. Dwarfish, with a plain face, pitted by smallpox scars, she had none of the newspaper infanta's physical attractions. And she showed no disposition, either before or after, to join the ranks of those alleged to be her kidnappers. So, notwithstanding comparable scenarios, Elizabeth Canning was not the poor man's Patty Hearst.

New Year's Day of 1753 she had off work, and the plans she made for spending it were typical. No gallivanting with admiring 'followers' (she had none); no high jinks at carnivals or fairgrounds. Just a long journey on foot from her master's house near Guildhall to her uncle's near the docks. She dressed in her cheap best: a purple gown, a white hat with green ribbons. She carried a little cash: her wages and her Christmas box.

The day passed in seasonable meals and quiet talk. Elizabeth left after supper, somewhere about nine. Her uncle and aunt escorted her part of the way home; when they turned back she had less than a mile to go. She pressed on into the unlit, but not yet empty, streets – and vanished. She did not reach her master's, nor her mother's house near by. For a month she was completely lost to her relatives and friends.

On 29 January, late in the evening, the widow Canning gaped at a strange creature who came hobbling to her door. Apparently an old woman; dirty, footsore, bent almost double, bleeding from one ear. It was moments before Mrs Canning grasped that her daughter had returned. Gone were the purple gown, the white hat, the green ribbons. Gone was the cash – the wages and the Christmas box. Gone, too, on closer inspection were her stays – female gear as regulation then as anachronistic now.

Gone, all gone – but where? Where had she been? And who had so misused her? Weary and sick though she obviously was, Elizabeth gave her answers there and then. To her mother and a growing band of sympathetic neighbours.

She got the words out slowly, painfully, amid many interruptions.

When I left uncle and auntie . . . ('Yes, yes, go on, go on.') Two men got hold of me. ('Where?') Along Moorfields. ('What sort of men?') Big, strong, they took my money, took my clothes right off my back. ('Oh, you poor love.') I screamed out and they gagged me. Hit me across the head. ('That's why you're bleeding.') No, that was a nail, escaping. ('A nail – in the open street?') No. Wait. Listen. I lost my senses awhile; next I knew they were dragging me along a road – a great wide road, somewhere out of the city. We reached a house, and they pulled me in. Three women were inside. They were . . . bad women. They asked me 'Will you go our way?' And I said 'No, I won't.' ('Oh, the innocent lamb.') Then one of the women took a knife and cut loose my stays. ('The bitch – I'd cut her eyes out.') They struck me, and pushed me up some stairs into a loft, all dark. ('Lord ha'mercy.') They never came near me four whole weeks, I saw none of them again. ('What did you eat? What did you drink?') There was a pitcher of water in the loft and a little bread. I got so weak I thought I'd die. At last, this afternoon, I managed to pull away a board from across the window, and climb through. That's when I tore myself on a nail. I walked along the road, asking the way, for miles and miles. ('What road was it, Lizzie?') I think the Hertford road.

LEFT: Elizabeth Canning; a contemporary engraving

One of her listeners spoke up, a young man of the world.

'The Hertford Road? A guinea to a farthing you were at Mother Wells's.'

So far Elizabeth had not mentioned anyone called Wells. But now she said she had heard that name during her ordeal at the house on the Hertford road.

Sometimes people making statements do great harm to themselves by revealing knowledge they could have gathered only at first hand. Like Mrs Major, hanged in 1934 for murdering her husband; she said to a Police Inspector, 'I did not know my husband had died from strychnine poisoning,' before being told that at the post-mortem strychnine had been found. Sometimes people making statements do great harm to others by adopting intentional or unintentional prompts. Like – it is possible, at least – Elizabeth Canning. When she swore to her statement before a magistrate, she included Mother Wells as though she had recalled the name spontaneously, unassisted. A warrant was issued, Mother Wells was raided, and everyone upon the premises was rounded up.

Elizabeth (who went on the raid) ignored Mother Wells herself, but picked out Mary Squires, a hideous gypsy hag, as the person who had robbed her. 'I never saw you in my life,' cried Mary Squires. 'Pray, madam, look at this face. If you have seen it once before, you must have remembered it, for God Almighty, I think, never made such another. Pray, madam, when do you say I robbed you?' 'On New Year's Day,' said Elizabeth. 'I was a hundred and twenty miles from this place then,' said Mary Squires.

Nonetheless, she was arrested and charged – with stealing Elizabeth's stays; not, for technical reasons, with a more serious offence. Mother Wells, accused of harbouring a thief, stood trial beside her. Each was convicted. Mother Wells was sentenced to be branded, Mary Squires to be hanged.

The sentence on the former was carried out forthwith. While preparations were being made to execute the latter, violent controversy arose over the verdicts. Was Elizabeth a kidnap victim or a consummate liar? Britain split into factions, 'Canningites' and 'Egyptians'. There were public disputes and arguments, private quarrels and fights. The Lord Mayor of London was a convinced 'Egyptian' and his

LEFT: Elizabeth Canning held captive by Mother Wells (left) and Mary Squires; a contemporary artist's impression

inquiries and representations tipped the scales. Mary Squires was pardoned and set free. Elizabeth was tried for perjury, found guilty, and transported.

On which side rests the truth? Who will be Canningites today and who today Egyptians? On either stance you are left to cope with devastating posers.

Say that you accept Elizabeth's tale as true. Why did she make no reference, in her initial version, to the unforgettable gypsy with a face so ugly and so weird that God Almighty never made such another? Why did the denizens of that house detain her when their accomplices had already grabbed her valuables? Why, indeed, did those accomplices, having secured their haul, trouble to drag an inert girl for such a distance? Whatever the women wanted ('Will you go our way?'), why did they not press her further when she was a captive? Why did she not try to escape until a month had passed? How did she survive so long upon so little? How did a starved, enfeebled girl trudge eleven miles to London? Why – unless it was a fact – did thirty-six witnesses swear that Mary Squires had been seen on New Year's Day in Dorset? Etcetera. Etcetera. Etcetera.

On the other hand, say that you regard Elizabeth's tale as false, believe that she made it up. What for? There is nothing in the evidence nor in her character to render any conjecture even faintly plausible. And if not at Mother Wells's for those four weeks, where was she?

The puzzles defy solution. The mystery endures.

The main line of kidnapping, which does not touch on cases like Canning and Hearst, used to be predominantly occupied with children. The very word contains that implication: the primary meaning of 'to kidnap' is 'to steal a child'. The stolen child being often a completely helpless infant. Although times past provide more illustrations, the most famous one is well within living memory.

Memories, of course, are proverbially short, but I for one should be surprised if anyone over fifty needed telling the essentials about Lindbergh. For those who are younger, they may be epitomized. His achievement was, as an unknown mechanic, to fly from New York to Paris – the very first transatlantic solo flight. His reward was to become the idol of America, and the unrivalled hero figure of the whole modern world. His tragedy is what now asserts claim to attention.

After his epoch-making feat with its unparalleled publicity, Lindbergh – twenty-five, agreeable, photogenic – was in demand from every side, and comfortably off. Presently he took a wife, a society lady. Presently they had a child, a son. To protect them all from well-meaning rubbernecks, he built a house on a site of his own selection – isolated amid rolling woods and lonely countryside. There they were safer from idle curiosity. But in greater danger from a calculating villain.

Such was Bruno Hauptmann, a thirty-six-year-old carpenter in the Bronx. Like everybody else, he read of Lindbergh's haven; like nobody else, he was fired with an infamous idea. He studied photographs of the house, sometimes joined the weekend sightseers. He watched out for, and collected, ancillary information: the number and denominations of the resident staff, the lay-out and occupancy of the different rooms. In his own attic he constructed a portable ladder, and meanwhile brooded endlessly over his nascent plan.

On 1 March 1932, he put it into effect.

The Lindbergh baby, then nineteen months old, had a nursery on the first floor. That night, at ten o'clock, the nursemaid returned from the servants' quarters to find his cot was empty. Perhaps with his mother, in the bathroom? No. Perhaps with his father, in the library? No. They searched the house, they searched outside. They did not find the child. But they found the marks and traces of his disappearance.

In the earth beneath the nursery window there were fresh indentations, as of a ladder's shafts. A few yards further along, abandoned, lay the ladder. On the window sill were muddy footprints – and a note, demanding fifty thousand dollars in small bills. 'After 2–4 days we will inform you where to deliver the money.'

It was not by any means an easy assignment for detectives. They were hindered rather than helped by Lindbergh's universal glory, and consequent closest scrutiny of every move they made. Cameras were above their heads; reporters underneath their feet; each day that passed without an arrest being made brought new thunderbolts of editorial criticism. But, though one may feel sympathy and make allowances, one must not disguise the fact that the local police bungled the job. They wasted time and energy on jurisdictional jealousies, they fought like Chicago Gangsters for territorial rights. They never uncovered the trail, far less unmasked the criminal. Small wonder that Lindbergh, distracted with grief, lost patience, and, despite official remonstration and advice, employed good-hearted amateurs as 'intermediaries'. There followed an extravaganza which mixed bloodcurdling melodrama with sidesplitting farce; notes under stones, messages sent by taxi, midnight meetings between strangers in a graveyard's gloom. Pledges were given – and broken. Hopes were raised – and dashed. At the end of these macabre antics the position was unchanged, save that, through an agent, Lindbergh had paid fifty thousand dollars to a stranger for some entirely false and fabricated information.

A few weeks later, on 12 May, the child's body, decomposed, was stumbled on by chance in woodland fifty yards from a road and four miles from his home.

Lindbergh, as was natural in a father, had attached less importance to the capture of the criminal than to the safe recovery of his son. The latter now a vanished dream, the former remained imperative if society was to be protected. Everything pointed to the recipient of the futile ransom. But nothing whatever pointed to his identity.

There was a long, long pause. A long wait for a sign. So long that the public put the case from mind, mentally marked 'unsolved'. But a breakthrough came at last. No bigger than a man's hand, it proved decisive.

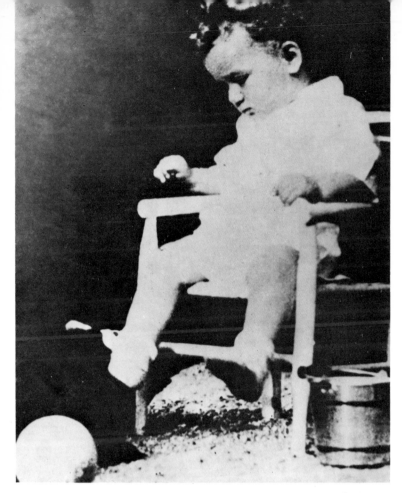

LEFT: The Lindbergh baby kidnapped at the age of nineteen months, 1 March 1932. His body was discovered in a wood a few weeks later

15 September *1934*. A petrol station somewhere in New York. A Dodge car drew in beside the pumps. Not a regular customer. One of the casuals served in dozens every day.

'Five gallons.'

The attendant took no particular notice of the driver. Just did as he was asked, and issued the payment slip. The driver gave him a ten-dollar note.

'Don't see many of those around nowadays,' said the attendant.

It was one of a series which the administration had lately ceased to print. The attendant perfunctorily pencilled on it the car's licence number.

A little later he took out – it was a ritual – a well thumbed, tattered list. Compared numbers on it with those of that day's takings. When he came to the ten-dollar note, he stared Almost incredulous. Stared again. Checked again with the list.

Telephoned the police.

The police of course had circulated to banks and traders the serial numbers of the Lindbergh ransom notes. Results had been disappointing, tardy and unfruitful. Many months elapsed before any came to light, and even these were few and far between. Most had made their first appearance in or near the Bronx. But they had not been able to narrow further their focus of enquiry. Now they could and did.

Minutes after the phone call, they knew who was the owner of the car. Minutes after that, they were interviewing him. Hauptmann bluffed about his possession of the tell-tale note, but the bluff was difficult to maintain. More so when they found, stowed away in his garage, ransom notes to the value of $14,000 – given him for safe keeping, he said, by a friend who had gone abroad. More so still when they found that a floorboard from his attic had been sawn away – and used as a portion of the kidnap ladder.

RIGHT: Charles Lindbergh (right) at the time of the trial of his son's kidnapper

The case against Hauptmann was really incontestible. At trial, defending counsel was forced to draw red herrings; unavailingly trying to cast suspicion on the nursemaid, and on the naïve delegate at the graveyard rendezvous. The machinery of American criminal law crawled along, as it often does, with maddening slowness, but it dispensed retributive justice in the end. Forty-nine months after the crime, nineteen after arrest, the do-it-yourself kidnapper and child murderer went to his own death in the electric chair.

The little Lindbergh baby did not die in vain. Across the globe, parents, especially if prominent and rich, were filled with anxiety and salutary alarm. The Lindbergh lesson registered and has lasted a long time, during which similar children have been that much safer. Not absolutely safe. I do not forget Peugeot's young son, seized in the Bois in daylight, with his brother and governess near by. (The motor magnate got him back by paying the sum demanded.) But, short of keeping them in prison rather than in parks, in frowning fortresses rather than in sunny playgrounds, how can small children, precious in a double sense, ever be rendered absolutely safe as long as the human race gives birth to creatures such as Hauptmann?

ABOVE: Hauptmann in court, 1 January 1935

BELOW: Four-year-old Eric Peugeot, son of the millionaire car manufacturer, is reunited with his mother after being released by his kidnappers

123

What has made this appear the 'kidnap generation' is not a marked rise in the kidnapping of children. It is the extension of kidnapping on a large scale to adults. Grown men and women, of substance and of standing, are major targets for contemporary predators.

This switch of subjects has synchronized with a switch of objects. In many cases, the latter is cause, the former is effect. Almost invariably, the kidnapping of a child is done for the purpose of extorting money whereas the kidnapping of adults has a wider scope. Frequently the motive is not financial but political. For example, to secure the release of political prisoners. In cases such as these a cash ransom may be demanded simultaneously; but more as a counter, for renunciation in a compromise. This political slant is the really novel feature of current kidnapping, more significant than any statistical variations. Though not unheard of earlier in Latin America and the Middle East, it was only in 1970 that the phenomenon hit the western world with stunning force.

Unlike its mighty next-door neighbour, Canada had been relatively free from any type of kidnapping. With all the more astonishment Canadians heard and read that, on 5 October 1970, the British Trade Commissioner accredited to their

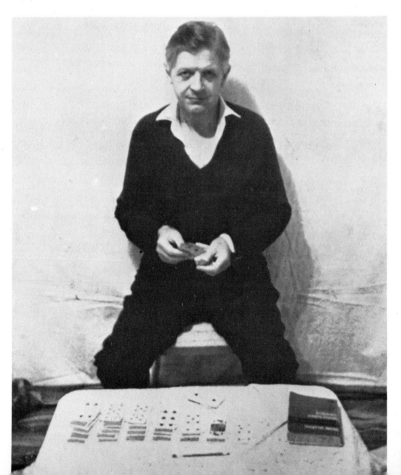

RIGHT: James Cross in captivity; this photograph was released by his kidnappers, 7 November 1970

land had been grabbed from his home at gunpoint by four armed men and driven away to an unknown destination. He was James Cross, forty-nine, a respected career diplomat. His kidnappers, who did not hide their provenance, were members of the FLQ (*Front de Libération Quebec*), a group which for some time had been threatening drastic action unless their separatist demands were satisfied. Breaches of the law by them had been expected. Some indeed had already been committed. But few had supposed that they would go as far as this. It was Canada's first political kidnapping.

If honest citizens in Canada were appalled, what should be said of their counterparts in Britain? They were in a state of shock. The venue contributed hardly less than the actual deed. It would have been bad enough for such a thing to happen to our man in Beirut, our man in Caracas. But our man in Montreal! Next we should be hearing of local autonomists kidnapping postmasters in Perth or Colwyn Bay.

The crime had serious repercussions reaching far beyond the individuals who were immediately involved. The Government of Canada was put into a quandary. The affair exacerbated its internal troubles while imposing a strain on its relations with the United Kingdom. British indignation combined with humane sentiment to encourage every possible step towards saving Mr Cross. The asking price had been precisely stated: More than twenty LFQ prisoners to be released from jail and flown out of Canada; more than £200,000 to be paid in gold to Cross's kidnappers (themselves to be granted safe conduct abroad). The Canadian Government could afford the latter; could it afford the former? What would be the long-term consequences of such a surrender to naked terrorism? Understandably, Ottowa foresaw grim possibilities. Prime Minister Trudeau forthrightly declared their attitude: 'You can't let a minority impose its view upon a majority by violence. . . . It is a difficult decision when you have to weigh a man's life in the balance, but certainly our commitment to society is greater than anything else.'

A statesmanlike and farsighted policy, but the policy-makers could never forget that simple, terrible fact – an innocent life might depend on their decision. They took care not to slam the door, and to stop it being slammed. They opened subterranean channels of communication. They stressed their hopes that a non-violent settlement could be arrived at. With Cross's 'execution' announced as imminent, they allowed FLQ's political manifesto, reciting grievances, to be broadcast on the state-owned radio. But battledores and shuttlecock were still in desperate play when something supervened which caused an even greater stir.

The FLQ kidnapped the Quebec Minister of Labour.

Pierre Laporte had been playing football with his young son and nephews when he was whisked away by a cluster of masked men. In a letter from captivity to the Premier of Quebec, he advocated a strategy different from that outlined by Trudeau. Urging first that the police should cease all efforts to find him, he went on: 'We are confronted by a well-organized escalation which will only end with the freeing of the political prisoners. After me it will be a third and then a fourth and then a fifth. If all the politicians are protected they will strike elsewhere – against other classes of society. Better to act quickly and thus avoid a useless blood-bath and panic.' This counsel, wise or not, was ultimately acted on; too late, however, to save that counsellor's own life.

BELOW: Pierre Laporte with his young son just before the kidnapping

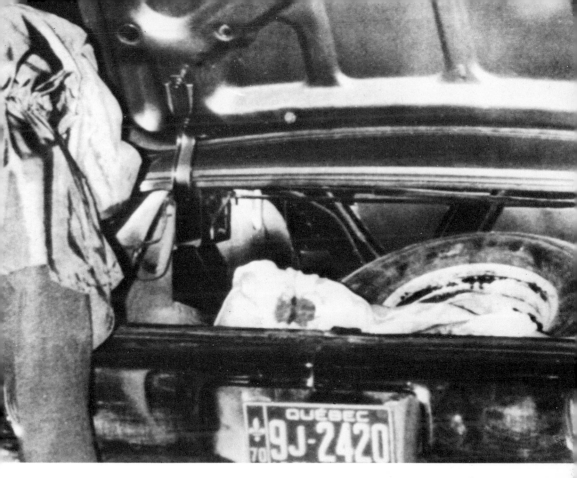

Laporte and Cross still being incarcerated, oblique negotiations still continued. On 14 October, FLQ issued an
announcement that both were alive and well. On 15 October,
the Canadian Government offered to free five FLQ prisoners
and no more. On 17 October, after a tip-off from his
murderers, the body of Laporte was found in the boot of a car
at St Huberts airport, twenty miles from Montreal. He had
been shot and strangled. It was Canada's first political killing
for more than a hundred years.

This dreadful news temporarily drew attention away from
Cross. But soon the implications that Laporte's fate had for
his put him more than ever in the forefront of men's minds.
There were despairing admissions by the police that they had
run out of leads. There were tentative hints by the Government of safe-conducts to the Caribbean. There were heart-
rending broadcasts made by Mrs Cross; hopefully to Cross
himself, beseechingly to his captors. Two more tense weeks
passed. At last there was a bargain struck.

ABOVE: The body of
Pierre Laporte was
found in the boot of a
car at St Huberts
airport outside
Montreal

127

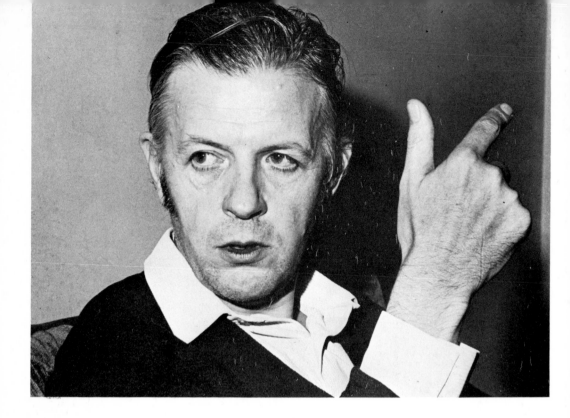

ABOVE: James Cross
after his release

The three kidnappers and four FLQ prisoners were proclaimed exiles for life. The Canadian Government put them on a plane for Cuba. In return the FLQ set free James Cross. He soon resumed his interrupted service to the Crown.

Accountancy is a wretched occupation when the figures are human figures and the totals writ in blood. Yet an accounting must be drawn up of the twin Canadian kidnappings if they are to teach a lesson for the future.

Two were taken. One was killed. One was spared (after protracted anguish for himself and others). The kidnappers gained an appreciable fraction – approximately a fifth – of their original requisition, plus a complimentary ticket to a place of their own choice.

That reckoning must be read against this background. The authorities, under a fearful test of nerve and judgement, began by boldly facing their prior obligation. As an elected Government, they took stand on the principle that they ought to safeguard their people as a whole and for all time before going to the rescue of separate individuals. However painful, however sacrificial, the principle might turn out in application. There was much to be said for adopting a tough line, but little to be said for adopting it and dropping it. If they had stuck to their guns after the murder of Laporte, they might – probably would – have consigned Cross to the same fate; they would have established, though, that what they said they meant, that they were not to be blackmailed or coerced by kidnapping. On the other hand, if they ever contemplated what one could call appeasement, it should surely have been put in operation straight away; thereby they would have lost less, not more, credibility and almost certainly preserved two lives instead of one.

I write my book with benefit of hindsight and detachment. Laporte wrote his letter without benefit of either.

'There came a time in the early or mid-seventies when hardly a single day of a single week could pass without news of a fresh kidnapping somewhere in the world.'

Today, 28 November 1975, I resumed work on this book as soon as I awoke. Before leaving my bed I wrote down the above sentence. While getting up I mused and pondered. Was it right?

At breakfast I turned the pages of the *Daily Express*. A headline caught my eye: MEAN KILLING OF KIDNAP GIRL. Naturally I read on with more than ordinary interest. A Swedish woman of twenty-six had been missing for three days. Her father, a wealthy farmer, had received a note demanding £40,000. The money was not paid, and the woman was murdered.*

This is not a contrived device on my part, a gimmick. It is a truthful report, a personal diary, of my morning. I only mention it as a timely instance of the point which I was making and, incidentally, of two others which I ought to make. That in kidnapping, utterly profitless killings may occur through anger, fright, or even sheer frustration. That, although adults are often kidnapped now for political reasons, the kidnapping of adults is not *exclusively* political. In their case, just as in the case of children, prospective financial gain still offers strong inducements. All members of a rich family are at perpetual risk. Lesley Whittle lost her life. The Getty grandson lost his ear. The Bronfman heir, though, escaped physically unhurt and the ransom money which had been paid was retrieved.

*A long shot, a gamble, that happened to come off? I purposely tried on a later date that week, with a different paper. *The Times* of 1 December. HINT OF RANSOM DEMAND FOR KIDNAP WOMAN headlined a dispatch from Milan about an abducted upper class Signora whose redemption price had been set at several million pounds to be paid over in diamonds abroad.

Young Samuel Bronfman was ideal kidnap bait. His father, boss of what the popular Press delighted in calling a whisky empire, had in that capacity amassed a personal fortune 'estimated to be in the billion-dollar range'. Samuel, lately graduated from a Massachusetts college, was just starting work in New York as a publisher's trainee. A lanky six foot three, with drooping moustache and a mop of curly hair, he was easily recognized and hence easily trailed. These qualifications would unite in recommending him to the selection committee of a snatch gang.

If you can detach your artistic from your moral perceptions – in the way that Sherlock Holmes did with Moriarty – you must to some extent admire the Bronfman operation. It was well conceived and well carried out to the brink of complete success. The kidnap itself, swift and sure, went unnoticed. The kidnappers henceforth prudently kept in the background, using the kidnappee to inform his father – by telephone at 2 am – that he was being held captive.

They tightened the screws shrewdly during the waiting period, promulgating the story, untrue as it transpired, that Samuel had been buried alive with air and water sufficient only for ten days. They loosened the screws adroitly after negotiations (via coded advertisements) by agreeing to accept one half of their original demand (for two million dollars). Then, with the money literally in the bag, their prudence evaporated and their luck ran out. The car collecting the dollars bore a licence number – Capone would have known better – which Bronfman Senior took note of. One of the minor parties in the conspiracy talked enough to narrow the scope of investigation. After the ransom was paid, they did not, as had been arranged, 'within hours' release the ransomed. And the telephone call, so useful earlier, boomeranged, leading to a Brooklyn apartment where Samuel lay bound and blindfolded and gagged, but otherwise, as Damon Runyon would have said, right as rain. Moreover, the dollars, carelessly stored like lumber, were near by.

It would seem a contradiction in terms to write of a 'happy' kidnap, but that of Samuel Bronfman had at least a happy ending. For all except – as a cautionary tale requires – the kidnappers. At the other extreme is the tale of Muriel

McKay. The infinite agony of so many innocent people, the unpenetrated mystery which surrounds the circumstances, make it both the most spine-chilling and most tragic case in the whole sombre history of kidnapping. Two other factors contribute to this melancholy distinction.

First, the victim's personality and background. A woman in middle life, of the upper middle class, married to a newspaper executive who adored her; charming chatelaine of a Wimbledon château, all her life accustomed to civilized comfort and civilized behaviour. Without Elizabeth Canning's habit of subordination, without Patty Hearst's insubordinate spirit, Muriel McKay was less equipped than either to withstand or adapt to the pressures always bearing on the kidnapped. Those pressures must have borne with special force on Mrs McKay because of the second factor that distinguishes her case.

LEFT: Muriel McKay

131

The character and background of the criminals. Arthur and Nizamodeen Hosein were brothers from Trinidad, who lived together at Rooks Farm, twelve acres of remotest Hertfordshire. Arthur, thirty-four, a British citizen, having done quite well for himself while an East End tailor, had bought the property on mortgage for £17,000. Nizamodeen, twenty-one, was without means or resources and faced a return home, when his visitor's permit expired, as penniless as he had been on the day he had set forth.

On the last Monday in December 1969, Alick McKay arrived home from his office at 7.45. He noticed that there had been some damage done to the front door, but not such as to cause him immediate alarm. The interior of the house wore an appearance of normality and occupation. The television was switched on, a coal fire burned cheerfully in the grate, the evening paper, opened, had been laid down on a chair. Outside, Mrs McKay's car was locked up in the garage, but Mrs McKay herself was nowhere to be seen.

Muriel, Muriel. The perplexed husband wandered from room to room. One or two were in disorder. Drawers pulled open. Furniture out of place. Strips of sticking plaster – what

132

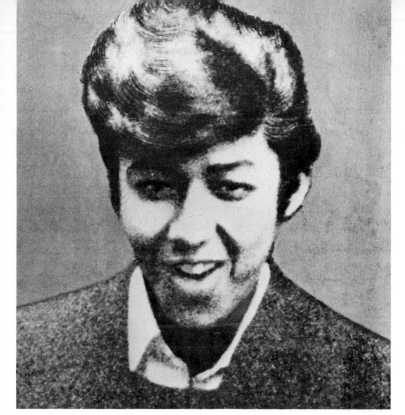

on earth for? – strewn about. Jewellery gone – ah, so there had been a robbery. Breaking and entering – accounted for the front door. Even so. Even so. Muriel, Muriel.

Most of us have experienced the trauma which is occasioned by the inexplicable absence of a loved one. Should I search the streets? Inform the police? Ring round the hospitals? When they are missing for no more than an hour. This was not only for an hour, or two, or six, or eight. Not only for a day, or week, or month. It was for ever.

Such a possibility, though it may flit to and fro, only strikes roots in the mind as time passes by. On that first night Alick McKay, having made every enquiry, taken every step, waited apprehensively – a street accident, perhaps? – but hardly doubting that presently he would know. If only – God forbid, God forbid – the worst. He cannot have contemplated that the worst would be as bad as it turned out.

At 1.30 am came a gleam of light – and a portent of the dark. The telephone ringing. She? She? Her own dear voice? But no. A man. Saying what you never expect to hear outside a thriller. A million pounds, we want a million pounds. And then hung up. A million pounds – for what? Mr McKay was

ABOVE: The secluded
McKay family home in
Wimbledon

left to guess, although the guess was easy. Almost unbelievably, Muriel had been kidnapped. By, it would seem, maladroit and rather stupid kidnappers. Who named an astronomical ransom utterly beyond Alick McKay's ability to meet. Who did not bother to ascertain his response. Who prescribed no method or details for the payment. Who pledged themselves to nothing whatsoever in return. The phone call raised the question (for those with leisure to ponder academic problems) whether it is better to deal with clever kidnappers or morons. Because it left Alick McKay no more able to locate or recover his wife than he had been before. It did not even give him an assurance that she was alive.

On Wednesday morning, however, a letter arrived for him at the house. Misleadingly, as is now known, posted in North London; unmistakably in Mrs McKay's handwriting. 'I am blindfolded and cold. Only blankets. Please do something to get me home. Please cooperate or I can't keep going.'

To me that letter suggests in part a *cri de coeur*, in part a product of dictation. Alick McKay was being begged to 'cooperate', presumably with the same man who, in subsequent phone calls, usually introduced himself as 'M3 of the Mafia'. But still ringing off abruptly, without contingent undertakings, without trying to set up machinery and arrange procedure. Only a threat to kill 'her' if the million pounds was not forthcoming. As the police smashed ice (which promptly re-formed) on the ponds round Wimbledon in an unavailing search, Alick McKay addressed the kidnappers through a published statement. 'What do you want from me? I am willing to do anything within reason to get my wife back.' He reinforced this statement with a television appeal in person.

Gradually advances were made – upon both sides. The original ransom call was traced to a telephone box at Epping. A fingerprint was detected on the letter from Mrs McKay. And, by agreement, under police control, suitcases (ostensibly packed with bank notes) were deposited in Epping Forest at unfrequented places which the ransom-seekers chose. None was collected (if the potential collectors suspected hidden watchers, they were right), but the last rendezvous proved the criminals' undoing.

Alert detectives observed a car drive three times towards the appointed spot and each time, after hesitating, drive away. The registered owner of that car was Arthur Hosein. By daybreak, a police cordon had been thrown around Rooks Farm.

BELOW: A massive police search was mounted at Rooks Farm, Hertfordshire, but Mrs McKay's body was never found

They picked up more than the two brothers at the farm. They picked up enough to prove twice over that they were the kidnappers. To take one item only: strips of sticking plaster corresponding exactly with those left behind at Wimbledon. And they took fingerprints, of course. Arthur's corresponded with that on Mrs McKay's letter.

But where *was* Mrs McKay? The Hoseins, sullen, hostile, remained silent.

The police thoroughly combed Rooks Farm. Outside as well as inside. Methodically, foot by foot. They swept. They thrust. They *dug*. Rooms, pigsty, fields. But not a trace of Muriel McKay, alive or dead. Not even an indication that she had ever been there. The Hoseins had had ample time to conceal – and to destroy.

Nonetheless, the brothers, who now started talking sufficiently to incriminate each other, were rightly charged with murder as well as kidnapping. And a jury rightly convicted them of both. Which exposed again the falsity of a popular belief that a charge of murder cannot stick unless a body is discovered.

It is hard to determine the source of this belief. It may derive from a misunderstanding of the term *corpus delicti*, which I have known used by policemen, lawyers – and also writers – as though it meant not all that goes to make a breach of the law, but the physical remains of the most terrible of breaches.

Several sensational trials in recent times have demonstrated that proof of murder does not require production of a corpse. Camb ('the Porthole Murderer'), who pushed Gay Gibson from a liner in mid-ocean. Onufrejczyc, the Polish soldier who settled in Wales and killed his business partner. But these trials did not shake what had become an article of faith, and the trial of the Hoseins has not done so either.

Both brothers went into the box. They passed the buck to one another for any blame that might attach ('I'm terrified of Arthur, he beats me up'; 'Nizam does things behind my back, he uses my car'). Both denied committing any offence of any kind. Both denied so much as setting eyes on Muriel McKay.

For an enquiry concluded, a case technically closed, the McKay kidnapping leaves a lot of questions open.

How did the kidnappers abduct her in the first place? By inducements? They could offer none. By deception – 'on some pretext', as the Attorney-General conjectured at their trial? One must then assume that they had accomplices, for Mrs McKay would not have trusted either of them an inch. By force? They could have ultimately overcome resistance – but would she not by struggle and by outcry draw attention in populated Wimbledon?

Why did they murder her? Maybe they did not plan to; maybe, a woman in frail health, she died from shock or exposure or neglect. No autopsy could be held to ascertain the cause of death.

How did they dispose of her after she had died? The possibilities are too grim for speculation.

In their separate jails, the loathsome brothers keep their secrets.

The word 'hi-jack' came into common usage with a restricted meaning. A hi-jacker, says the Concise Oxford Dictionary (1952 edition), is a person who preys on bootleggers, appropriating and profiting by their illicit liquor (for example, Bugs Moran with Al Capone). But today it has a far wider connotation, and no account of kidnapping can possibly ignore hi-jacking as an up-to-date fast growing development.

Hi-jacking in its contemporary sense does not really depart from the ancient kidnap formula. It is still the seizure and detention of individuals in the hope and expectation of trading their release for the fulfilment of demands. Only the application of this formula has changed; use is made of novel agencies, new instruments. As the horse was superseded by the motor car, the motor car has been superseded by the aeroplane. A quicker getaway, a larger haul of hostages, a stronger, but still mobile, fortress from which to negotiate.

Hi-jackers seldom project attractive personalities. Characteristic specimens have tapering heads, simian features, stubbly cheeks and (optionally) ragged beards; like male film extras for a scene set in the Baghdad slums. But the day came which produced an exception, a surprise. She was Leila Khaled. Yes, a girl – and what a girl! Flashing, dazzling smile; limpid, inviting eyes; slim, elegant even in her battledress of blouse and jeans – her pictures revived for older men the younger Lena Horne. A peach, an eyeful, a smasher, a dish – according to the vocabulary of your generation. Brains, too; a schoolteacher by profession before she gave up to become a wholetime Palestine guerrilla. Her looks and exploits quickly made her the idol of Arab youth, and an object of reluctant admiration in the West. Not only a hold-up, also a pin-up, girl. But it was not as such that Leila Khaled saw herself, nor was it how she wanted to be seen. She was a warrior dedicated to her cause, in the tradition of Joan of Arc and Boadicea. Arguably she, also, descried visions and heard voices. 'If I am called upon to do it again,' she said, after hijacking a Boeing 707 to Syria, 'I shall do it again. It is my duty.'

She did it again – or tried to. Leila Khaled did not requite Western admiration with affection. 'The West is a friend of Israel,' she declared, 'and friends of my enemies are my enemies.' She must have felt that she was striking both at her enemies and at her enemies' friends when, in the late summer of 1970, she boarded another Boeing 707. One in the fleet of

BELOW: Leila Khaled training with her guerilla group in Jordan

the El Al Airline, a plane bound for the United States carrying 145, including Americans, British, Germans as well as Israelis. Leila Khaled had a male confederate with a gun, and hand grenades secreted on her and about her.

The plane stopped off at Amsterdam, then headed for New York. Over the North Sea, approaching the English coast, the

LEFT: Leila Khaled

BELOW: The wreckage of the BOAC VC10 blown up by Palestinian guerillas on a desert airstrip in Jordan after the release of Leila Khaled, September 1970

Arab pair suddenly sprang into violent action. Her confederate, gun pointing, and she, grenade at the ready, endeavoured to make their way into the pilot's cabin. No doubt to order him to switch to some point in the Middle East. Confusion broke out in the crowded aircraft – shouts, wails, expostulations – which may have distracted or temporarily unnerved her companion. As he floundered, a member of the crew instantly shot him dead. Leila Khaled pressed on, cool and resolute, but was grasped and pinioned by a plucky passenger. Asked afterwards how he did it, he engagingly explained: 'Just a few minutes before, I had had a gin and tonic.' But for that Wyatt Earp of the air – but, perhaps, for that gin and tonic – the plane and its entire cargo of lives might well have perished. As it was, they made an emergency landing at Heathrow, and the glamorous hi-jacker passed into British custody.

The Government took a long time deciding what to do with her. Superficially it was a simple issue. She had patently committed a crime, and hence she should be charged. But Leila Khaled's friends created complications. On a desert strip in Jordan at that time stood two aircraft with Israeli, German and British citizens aboard. Guerillas loaded these aircraft with dynamite; a single spark and they could be blown sky-high. The guerillas threatened to apply that spark. Let Leila go – or else!

Through the month of September continued an interplay of pressures. The age-old kidnap dilemma in ultra-modern form. London held a hostage, Jordan hostages. Jordan, in this situation, held more power. Terms were agreed, a double release was effected. The Israelis, Germans, British, safely left their powder-kegs. Safely from captivity emerged Leila Khaled.

She had been promised transportation to wherever she wished. No available airline, though, would consent to fill a seat with so hot a property. Finally the RAF gave her a flight – to Cairo. Leila Khaled was back in business.

The following month she got married – to another guerilla. The following year she published her autobiography. I last read of her training revolutionaries in Japan. I question whether she would ever qualify as a geisha.

She might yet become Miss World, however, or anyhow Miss Kidnap.

One must guard against falling under the spell of a prepossessing exterior (I am conscious of falling often myself into the opposite trap). There has been no lack of comely criminals: Peter Griffiths, Richard Loeb, Ruth Ellis, Patrick Mahon. Few quite so comely as Leila Khaled. Few quite so ruthless, desperate, and fearless.

Happily for their own fair name and the comfort of us all, she has not so far had many imitators among her sex. But the practice of hi-jacking, albeit on the whole by men, gathers rather than loses its momentum. The papers this morning (7 December 1975) once again bear topical witness to that fact. And to another fact also: there are signs that, in one secondary respect, the procedure of the hi-jackers is becoming regressive. They are turning to machines less technologically advanced. This could be the result of increased security on airfields. Whether or no, on the front page the headline reminds us that yesterday was the FIFTH NIGHT FOR TRAIN PRISONERS – a reference to the coup in Holland by the South Moluccans.

We have seen almost every variety of kidnapping sideshow. We have seen some elaborately staged kidnapping productions. How long before we see the kidnapping spectacular?*

*Not long. Arab guerillas – Leila Khaled's lot – successfully swooped on the OPEC chieftains at Vienna in good time for inclusion. Among the bandits – meanly stultifying me – was a girl.

CONVICTED CRIMINAL: "Harley Street, John!"

5.

CRIME WITHOUT RESPONSIBILITY?

PLEAS OF INSANITY

Lieutenant Holt
Colonel Rutherford
Ronald True
Dale Nelson
Leopold and Loeb
Harry Thaw

When I was a small child, living with my parents in Manchester where I was born, we spent our holidays every summer at St Annes, a demure, pleasant resort to the south of gaudy Blackpool. Between them lay undulating sandhills, alternate humps and hollows stretching for a mile. Children at St Anne's went there to picnic and to play. Each group would select some hollow as its base, changing daily, for there was nothing to distinguish them – sparse clumps of thin grass, soft grainy sand, the motor roadway on the east, on the west the sea. No reserves, no signs saying 'Trespassers Forbidden'. You chose the hollow you preferred and settled in. One year, though, a new, unwritten law prevailed. A particular hollow had been made taboo. For no visible reason. It still seemed like the others. Indeed, you could only tell it by the landmark of a tram stop. But 'that place' was put strictly out of bounds. Without explanation. Mothers and nannies gossiped among themselves, but in voices so low one could hardly hear. Collating scraps however, over several weeks, I gathered somebody named Holt had done something dreadful in that hollow. Exactly what it was I did not learn for several years.

'Eric' to his many friends, Frederick Rothwell Holt was both a hero and a victim of the First World War. As a Territorial officer, he had been called up at the outset and spent the ensuing winter in the trenches. In the spring, as a lieutenant he had fought at Festubert and emerged from that inferno shell-shocked. He was invalided out of the Army, gradually returning to civilian life among the younger social set of a northern town. In 1918 he met a beautiful young woman with whom he fell in love and who fell in love with him. Her name was Kitty Breaks. She represented herself to be single, and behaved as though she were. Actually she was living apart from her husband after a brief, unhappy experience of wedlock. This fact she disclosed to Eric Holt only when they were already deep in an affair. Holt does not appear to have been disquieted or dismayed. A woman's marriage may act, not as a restraint, but as an aphrodisiac on an extra-matrimonial partner.

On 23 December 1919, Kitty took a room for herself at a hotel within walking distance of the sandhills of St Anne's. She dined alone; after dinner she went out. She had an

PAGE 142: A contemporary cartoonist's comment on the reprieve of Ronald True; the *Evening News*, 13 June 1922

assignation with Holt, who had travelled with her by train but had got off at a station a few minutes down the line. Early next day, Kitty's dead body, pierced by three bullets, was found upon the sandhills. A revolver, a pair of gloves, and adjacent footprints showed that Eric Holt had kept his assignation.

Murderer and murdered each excited sympathy. The shattered soldier and his lovely lady – human sacrifices to the greedy god of war. That at least was a common impression as the sensational tale unfolded. Sensation reached a climax, of course, at Holt's trial, when he was defended by Sir Edward Marshall Hall.

LEFT: Sir Edward
Marshall Hall (right)

Marshall Hall was then himself approaching, if not the climax, the zenith of his remarkable career. There were still triumphs waiting for him well ahead: Madam Fahmy in 1923, Alfonso Smith (the 'Stella Maris case') in 1926. But 1919 was to be his *annus mirabilis*, embracing as it did the acquittals, both against heavy odds, of Ronald Light (the 'Green Bicycle case') and Harold Greenwood. But against Holt the odds were more than heavy; they were overwhelming. The Attorney-General, Sir Gordon Hewart, spelt that out in measured accents. 'The gloves – his gloves – how did they come to be there? The revolver – his revolver – how did that come to be there? The footprints – his footprints – how did they come to be there?' It was asking more than could be answered satisfactorily even by Marshall Hall in his finest form. If there was to be any chance of saving Holt's neck – an extremely remote and slender chance at best – there was only one possible defence. Insanity. A defence lent a little colour because a grandfather of Holt's had been insane. That defence contented Holt. Less so Marshall Hall. But the dynamic advocate, having bowed to the inevitable, fought it with all his might every inch of the way. He raised the issue *before* trial, calling medical evidence that Holt's mental state *at that moment* made him unfit to plead. A jury rejected *this* contention. He raised the issue *during* trial, calling medical evidence that Holt's mental state *at the time of the crime* made him not responsible. Another jury rejected *this* contention. He raised the issue in the Court of Criminal Appeal, where he took the exceptional course of applying for leave to call fresh evidence – that of a doctor who, on reading newspaper reports, remembered once treating Holt for syphilis, a disease that often leads to general paralysis of the insane.

The Lord Chief Justice, Lord Reading, presiding, invited Marshall Hall to state, in broad terms, the grounds for his application. Counsel did so – and seized the opportunity to indicate the basis and nature of the whole appeal.

'I am going to ask you to consider, in this year of 1920, the whole question of insanity and the subject of mental disease. It is time the question was settled. I am going to show that, owing to a condition of mind which was due partly to heredity and partly to syphilis, the appellant killed Mrs Breaks as a result of uncontrollable impulse.'

146

Lord Reading was put at once on the alert.

'What is the proposition which you say is to be added to the M'Naghten case, or by which you say that case is to be modified?'

Out of M'Naghten's case sprang the so-called M'Naghten Rules which, from 1843 to 1957, governed the scope of insanity as a defence in English law. Some other legal systems borrowed or adopted them. Before going further into Holt's case, or on to others, a few words about those Rules are therefore requisite.

Although reluctant to quote myself, I cannot summarize their general effect better than I did in an earlier book, *A Century of Murderers*, when I wrote: 'They declared that a man's abnormal state of mind did not exempt him from liability for a crime *unless* he did not know what he was doing or did not know that what he was doing was wrong.' (The onus of proof in this respect properly rested not on the Crown but on the accused.)

Battle raged for many years round the M'Naghten Rules. Those who wished to maintain and retain them versus those who wished to erode or erase them. The legal concept versus the medical concept of insanity. Often unduly personalized into lawyers versus doctors (more accurately, lawyers versus psychiatrists). But really this battle should never have been joined. Law and medicine have different ends. Medicine attempts to define *insanity*, the law to define *conditions which must be satisfied if someone is to be excused from criminal responsibility*. No conflict can occur while each remains within its province. But the psychiatrists worked long and hard to burst out from theirs, to blur the frontiers between the clinic and the court where, contrary to some presumptions, not least their own, they do not enter the box to announce decisions, only to give opinions that may – or may not – assist the jury that has to decide. 'You are not bound in any way,' Mr Justice Finnemore told the Christie jury, 'by the views expressed by the doctors, except to give them careful consideration as evidence in this case.'

The gulf between psychiatric doctrine and the M'Naghten Rules has been usefully formulated by Lord Denning. 'The M'Naghten Rules lay the emphasis on the man's knowledge, not his will power. . . . The test applied by doctors in judging insanity denies the distinction between a man's knowledge and his will power.' The Rules do not admit 'uncontrollable' or 'irresistible' impulse as a defence. (Whether an impulse so described constitutes insanity by medical definition is immaterial.) The exclusion was wise; it is hard to avoid confusion between what is 'uncontrollable' and what is simply uncontrolled. As Kenny says in his classic *Outlines of Criminal Law*:

The world is full of 'warped' men and women in whom there exists some taint of insanity, but who nevertheless are readily influenced by the ordinary hopes and fears that control the conduct of ordinary people. To place such persons beyond the reach of such curative and deterrent methods of treatment as are now available to the courts would not only be to violate the logical consistency of our theory of crime, but would also be *a cause of actual danger to the lives and property of their neighbours.*

RIGHT: The *Daily News*, 28 February 1920

0 MORE VOTERS.

Sanctioned in mons.

ACY SPEECH Y ASTOR.

men voters will be te of the United King- ich passed the Second se of Commons yester- ision is placed on the proposal is to reduce for women voters from s to place them on an

Rother Valley, Yorks), reading of the Repre- ple Bill, explained that he Franchise Act, 1918. ranchise on women on erms as men, first by imit of 30 years, and me limit as for men, sought to secure poli- een the sexes and all ng the occupational the qualification of d by placing the whole xes for Parliamentary nt purposes on the ence, with the excep- ty electors. he age of women d the effect of keeping great mass of the in- men of the country. one in fifteen women The Bill would prevent oters from losing their tion if they had not 1. It gave the elector nce only in any con- or she had a residen- the qualification would esidence and manhood Women were the equals nce and ability, and uch common sense as he franchise. The Bill ration fee for students

T ATTITUDE.

he Government, said g the age for women vould be to increase out 5,000,000 persons, than 13,000,000 men ian 13,000,000 women le. It was estimated t half a million more

HOLT FOUND GUILTY.

SENTENCE OF DEATH IN SANDHILLS TRIAL.

'GLOATING WOMEN.'

SIR E. MARSHALL - HALL'S STRONG PROTEST.

From Our Own Correspondent.

MANCHESTER, Friday.

After an absence of 55 minutes the jury at the Manchester Assizes this evening returned a verdict of wilful murder against Frederick Rothwell Holt, ex-lieutenant, who shot Mrs. Kathleen Breaks, of Brad- ford, on the sandhills at St. Anne's on Christmas Eve. Holt received the death sentence with an air of indiffe- rence. He had nothing to say in reply to the usual invitation, and, put- ting his hands in his pockets, he turned on his heels and went below.

The only time he has shown the slightest sign of emotion during the whole of the five days' proceedings was to-day, when Sir Edward Marshall-Hall made an impas- sioned speech for the defence. On four occasions when counsel reefrred to the affection which the murdered woman had for Holt prisoner's eyes filled with tears, whic hhe quickly wiped away.

Sir Edward, at the opening of his ad- dress, said: "It makes one's heart ache to look around and see a court packed with women until they can hardly move. It makes me feel sorry for the femininity of this country that they should come here in dozens day by day just to gloat over the troubles of a man on trial for his life."

Mr. Justice Greer's summing up was against the prisoner, and little surprise was occasioned at the jury's verdict.

SPEECH FOR DEFENCE.

Ex-Lieut. Holt.

NEW

Suprer

MR. WI

The text of to the Adria White Paper

The import text of the la President Wil a proposal has previous propo Slavia negotia a clean sheet.

THE DEC

Lord Cur S

The corres begins with tl memorandum and signed by Eyre Crowe, w can representa forth the pe already in agre son. The Wils dary in Istria, of Fiume " wa League of Nati

The agreemer nomous Zara, tions (but wit Union), gave I groups of isla and offered her with full sovei

Beyond thes tories to the m They considere garded Zara v Italy's demanc diplomatic rela jected the Ita dor " along t Fiume as run known consid nomics, and They also rej

That is the nub, and the rejection of 'uncontrollable impulse' was one of the greatest safeguards provided by the Rules. Yet it was this flank of the fortress, which had so long withstood assault, that was ultimately breached. Not simply through bombardment from the box, though that contributed, but through legislation, passed by politicians who were a prey either to sheer ignorance or to the pressure of the psychiatric lobby composed of misguided do-gooders and impractical theoreticians. The 1957 Homicide Act prescribed that 'where a person kills . . . he shall not be convicted of murder if he was suffering from such abnormality of mind . . . as substantially impaired his mental responsibility for his acts.' Thus creating the defence known as 'diminished responsibility'. Thus driving a coach and four through the M'Naghten Rules.

Had such a defence been open to him, Holt might well have got away with 'diminished responsibility'. But there was then no indulgent Homicide Act, and the Court of Criminal Appeal declined Marshall Hall's invitation to 'consider the whole question of insanity'. They considered, as they were required to do, established law and its application to the case before them. 'The M'Naghten Rules,' said Lord Reading, 'must be observed' – and the Rules were not suspended for syphilis or shell-shock. So a noose claimed the survivor of St Annes and Festubert.

Absence of ascertainable motive always tends to sustain a plea of insanity. Imagination may speculate, but Holt's motive, now as then, remains obscure. No obscurity shrouds that of a warrior of higher rank who had been tried for murder several months before. The motive prompting him patently was jealousy, coupled, as so often, with misconceived revenge.

Late one evening in the January following the Armistice, a man wearing officer's uniform, decorated with the ribbon of the DSO, knocked at the front door of a house in London's Holland Park. The parlour-maid who opened it did not know him. She stood wondering, waiting till he spoke.

'I want to see Major Seton.'

'*Major* Seton? This is Sir Malcolm Seton's house.'

'But Major Seton is with him tonight, I've been given to understand.'

The maid hesitated.

'Who shall I say it is, sir?'

The maid asked him to wait in the hall while she went upstairs. Sir Malcolm and his wife and his cousin, Major Seton, were sitting over their coffee, after dinner.

'To see *me*?' said the major. 'What is his name?'

'Colonel Rutherford.'

The Major looked astonished.

'Shall I—' Lady Seton began, half rising.

'No, no, I'll go. Can't think what he wants, though. Or how he knew I was here.'

'Who is he, Miles?'

'Oh, an old friend. But I hadn't even heard that he was back from France.'

'Bring him in here, Miles.'

'Oh no.'

The Major left them. Lady Seton and Sir Malcolm went on chatting. Presently they heard, in quick succession, several sharp reports. Exchanged incredulous glances.

'It can't be—!'

They ran downstairs. The first thing they saw was the Major lying on the floor, wounded beyond speech. The second was a stranger in khaki, standing upright, rigid, like a well-trained guardsman at attention. The third was a pistol lying on a table.

'You have killed him!' Lady Seton cried.

'Yes,' replied the stranger. 'I only wish I had another bullet for myself.'

Sir Malcolm hurried out to fetch a doctor. When he returned Lady Seton was trying to aid a man past aid; the stranger was sitting quietly holding his head in his hands.

There are many stories of officers shooting privates who have refused to fight, of privates shooting officers who have incurred unpopularity. All under the cover and in the stress of war. But for one senior officer in peacetime deliberately to seek out another in order to murder him is an event demanding some better explanation than a messroom quarrel or a disciplinary dispute. And one soon came to light which accounted for, if it did not justify or palliate, the killing of Major Seton by Colonel Rutherford. The originating cause was the sorrow and distress of a third party – Mrs Rutherford.

OPPOSITE: The *Daily Graphic* reports the murder of Major Miles Seton, 15 January 1919

150

£1,000 Insurance. This copy of the "Daily Graphic" carries a Free Insurance of £1,000 undertaken by the Ocean Accident and Guarantee Corporation, Limited. (See page 2.)

PEACE CONFERENCE SURPRISES.

LONDON EDITION

THE DAILY GRAPHIC

One Penny

LONDON: WEDNESDAY, JANUARY 15, 1919.

No. 9079.—Vol. CXVII.

Registered as a Newspaper.

CRYSTAL PALACE AS "CLEARING HOUSE." | MILITARY TRAGEDY IN LONDON.

MAJOR MILES CHARLES SETON, AUSTRALIAN MEDICAL CORPS, THE VICTIM OF THE TRAGEDY. (Elliott and Fry.)

SIR MALCOLM SETON, AN INDIA OFFICE OFFICIAL, AT WHOSE HOUSE THE TRAGEDY OCCURRED. (Elliott and Fry.)

Yesterday the Crystal Palace began its mission as the chief demobilisation base for the men of the forces. Large numbers of men can be dealt with there at one time, and a considerable "speeding up" has begun. 1. On arrival at the Palace the men hand in their papers before being passed through the rest of the routine. 2. The big dinner party. Tommy frequently arrives hungry, and is provided with a satisfactory meal, which (3) he thoroughly enjoys. By the end of the present week it is anticipated that half a million men in all will have been demobilised. ("Daily Graphic" photographs.)

At the West London Police Court yesterday Lieutenant-Colonel Norman Rutherford, D.S.O., was charged with the wilful murder of Major Miles Charles Seton, who was found shot at the residence of Sir Malcolm Seton, 13, Clarendon Road, Holland Park, on Monday night. Colonel Rutherford, who won the D.S.O. for evacuating wounded under shell fire, was remanded. 1. No. 13, Clarendon Road. 2. Detective Inspector Percy Savage, who arrested Colonel Rutherford and gave evidence. 3. After the police court proceedings—the accused officer was removed from the court in a taxi.

Colonel Rutherford was domestically difficult. Quick-tempered, possessive, abnormally suspicious, with a streak of tyranny which could take cruel forms, he engendered such continuous tensions in the marriage that his charming wife led a miserable life. A woman so placed yearns for a trusted friend, one she can not only confide in but can lean on. However misguidedly, however riskily, she often chooses to rely on male strength. Miles Seton, the Colonel's friend and a frequent visitor to his home, had been Mrs Rutherford's natural confidant. There was no romantic attachment; that would have disqualified Seton for his loftier role. In moments of privacy afforded by her drawing room, she poured into his sympathetic ear a chronicle of injuries at her husband's hands or from his lips – or from his pen, for Seton did not cease to call when the Colonel was on duty at the front. Rutherford learnt of these calls, and put the worst construction on them. Having made up his mind that Seton must have seduced his wife (despite her vehement denials when impugned), he felt that only one proceeding could redeem his honour. That line of thought culminated in the hall of Sir Malcolm Seton's house in Holland Park. I do not think there is any question about that. I entirely disregard Rutherford's protests that he never doubted his wife's fidelity. I am fully convinced that he set out that night to shoot the man whom he supposed to be her lover. But even had his supposition been correct, it would have availed him nought as a defence. The *crime passionel* has no place in English law, as was to be demonstrated later to Ruth Ellis. What Rutherford had done was literally indefensible. And when someone has done what cannot be defended those concerned with his defence consider his state of mind.

It is an instructive exercise to split the component parts of the insanity plea put forward on behalf of Rutherford. The fits of temper (usually vented on his wife). A habit of fidgeting (as barristers fiddle with the tape on their briefs). Bouts of depression (which now and again afflict the most euphoric). The 'maddening' irritation of chronic dermatitis. The undermining plague of permanent insomnia. And of course – what was really an appeal *ad misericordiam* – the effect of long devoted service under fire (an excuse for civilian violence as automatic in its time as the flicks and the telly were to be in theirs). None of these factors could be seriously regarded as causes or symptoms even of 'medical' insanity. But taken together they might appear a commonsensical foundation for what analysis reveals as a nonsensical contention.

A superstructure of two eminent alienists who, drawing on that material and their examination of 'the patient' and on their vast stores of academic learning, pronounced that Rutherford was insane according to the M'Naghten Rules. Either he did not know what he was doing when, with a pistol, he was hunting Major Seton. Or he did not know that it was wrong when he shot him down.

Did the Old Bailey jury treat this contention with the contemptuous scorn it merited? They did not. Within five minutes they decided to endorse it. Colonel Rutherford had put himself upon his country, and his country had been generous in response.

At a quick glance, Rutherford's case is on all fours with Holt's. Holt had experts, Rutherford had experts. Holt had been a gallant soldier, Rutherford another. Holt had a mad grandfather, Rutherford a mad aunt. Why, then did Holt go to the gallows and Rutherford to Broadmoor?

Largely because public opinion, embodied in the jury, was readier to take a lenient line with Rutherford. Whatever the law may say, ordinary citizens do subconsciously make allowances for anything that they regard as a *crime passionel*.

Holt did not altogether fit into this fluid category. He had killed his sweetheart, but for reasons far from clear. If it could have been shown that he had killed her out of jealousy, that would have stamped his as a *crime passionel* – and might well have swayed the verdict in his favour. Rutherford's – though he himself, outside the court, disowned it as such – was a *crime passionel* of the traditional type. Hence an anxiety as far as possible to spare him. Hence the only available verdict that would do so.

There is little that society will not accept as means when it has already collectively willed the end.

Ronald True, if he could know, would swell with snobbish pride at rubbing shoulders, if only in a catalogue of crime,

with such as Colonel Rutherford and Lieutenant Holt. First, they were entitled to the ranks they claimed, whereas 'Major' True was an impudent impostor. Second, Holt's crime held an intriguing mystery and Rutherford's a certain sombre dignity, while True's crime was shabby and sordid to an extreme. One need not, for present purposes, enlarge upon it. Enough to say that, in March 1922, he spent the night at the flat of a London prostitute, and murdered her there so that, in the morning, he could run off with her small change and her paltry jewels. And that the evidence against him was conclusive.

Once again the stark alternatives. A verdict of insanity or a sentence of death.

True's case however, as presented in court, differed in one important regard from his predecessors'. His defenders were able to call an expert whose opinion commanded quite exceptional respect. Dr Norwood East was not a professional pundit, spouting polysyllabic passages from scholastic theses. He had had a long and notable career in the prison service studying men, not assimilating abstractions. As Medical Officer at Brixton (to which jail True was remanded) he had observed the accused day by day for many weeks, not merely for an hour or two in formal 'consultation'. Without instructions or retainer, he had volunteered the view that True was certifiable, and – more pertinent – incapable of distinguishing moral right from moral wrong.

East's questioning by Sir Richard Muir, the prosecutor, is a fine example of cross-examination rounding up a fugitive (True) from the M'Naghten Rules.

East was on record as adopting the 'medical' rather than the 'legal' attitude to the Rules. No one would have dreamt of challenging his probity, but there is such a thing as honest bias. Muir thought that East's attitude should be made known to the jury and, in making it known, he won an unexpected bonus.

'Is it your view that the M'Naghten Rules are the proper rules, or that they ought to be relaxed?'

The answer was there for the asking. Muir went on.

'You have advocated a revision of the Rules?'

'No, I do not think I have, because my difficulty has always been to offer an alternative.'

Muir doubled his stake.

'I do not quite know what that means.'

It paid off.

'I do not see,' said East, 'how far you can relax them *safely*.'

Muir carefully forestalled disagreement about the point in issue.

'The question we are upon is whether he knew at the time he did this act that it was an act punishable by law?'

'Yes.'

An understanding thus secured, Muir confronted East with the undisputed facts one by one, which magnified their effect.

'He arranged the pillows to look as if the woman was in bed. Isn't the obvious reason that he desired to conceal what he had done?'

Dr East never quibbled, never wriggled.

'Yes,' he said.

'Then he removed the body from the bedroom into the bathroom?'

'Quite so.'

'Wasn't that obviously to conceal from anyone looking into the bedroom that he had committed the act?'

'I should think so.'

'Then he told the daily maid, when she arrived, that her mistress was asleep, and not to disturb her?'

'Yes.'

'Was that for the purpose of winning him time to get away?'

'Probably.'

Muir had got enough now to encapsulate.

'All those acts, committed on the spot and immediately after the crime, were consistent with a desire to conceal the fact of murder?'

'Yes.'

'And his connection with it?'

'Yes.'

Muir's next was a dispatching shot.

'Does it not show he knew what he had done was punishable by law?'

The straightforward witness conceded that was so. An intelligent jury decided that was so. They found True guilty –

guilty of wilful murder, without any saving clause about his state of mind. The judge imposed the penalty which was then prescribed.

But True's case, as a subject open for decision, did not end with May the Lord Have Mercy on Your Soul. Lesser powers than the Almighty intervened.

I am not referring to the Court of Criminal Appeal. An appeal *was* made to that tribunal – and dismissed. Exit the judiciary. Enter the executive.

It is a settled principle of English common law, far far more ancient than the M'Naghten Rules, that people shall not be executed when they are insane. Insane *at the time proposed for execution*, as distinct from *at the time when the crime was committed* (though one would expect insanity either at both times or at neither). If the Home Secretary has any information suggesting that a person under sentence of death may be insane, he has statutory powers to order an enquiry into that person's *present* state of mind. It is not discretionary. It is not permissive. It is mandatory. The 'information' about True was the evidence of Norwood East and others at the trial, which would be conveyed to the minister by the judge. The Home Secretary set up a commission of three doctors who unanimously reported that True was insane. That did not – necessarily – run counter to the jury's verdict for they were focussing on a different time and on a different point: whether True was 'medically' sane, not whether he was criminally responsible. The practical effect, however, was the same as if the jury had pronounced that he was not. The commission left its progenitor without an option. The Home Secretary granted a reprieve.

True spent the remainder of his life – nearly thirty years – in Broadmoor. He died, of natural causes, at the age of sixty-one. In theory he could have been hanged if he 'recovered' sanity, but that was never really a viable proposition – any more than was another attempt to hang John Lee of Babbacombe. Which proved to be just as well for True. Because at Broadmoor – where he became immensely popular, a model inmate who managed the canteen – he never manifested any symptom of derangement. Indeed, by the test of rational behaviour, some think that he came off better than the superintendent.

Across wide seas and into other lands, the M'Naghten Rules have shown themselves particularly exportable in a westerly direction. To Canada, for instance, where they are enshrined in Section 16 of the Criminal Code, and where they thus exerted salutary authority over a case of multiple murder not so long ago.

Every man, unless supplied with objective guidelines, judges sanity subjectively, taking himself as the mental norm. When people say, as they often do, 'I can't imagine *anyone sane* doing anything like that,' what they mean is 'I can't imagine *myself* doing anything like that.' Few of us could imagine ourselves doing what was done by one individual in British Columbia during a weekend late in the summer of 1970.

Dale Nelson was a *regular* guy (sociable, jolly, hail-fellow-well-met) only at intervals – when he had gone on a spree. At other times he was introverted, taciturn, even surly; without enemies but equally without close friends among his widely scattered neighbours in West Creston. But always he was an *ordinary* guy without any exceptional characteristics or proclivities. No one ever thought of him as a potential man of mark. No one ever thought of him as a potential criminal either.

He was thirty-one, living with his wife and three young children in a wooden shack on a dirt road which meandered through an expanse of open bush. He made a precarious living as a freelance logger, employed, when jobs were going, by local companies. His family liabilities might have been better met through an occupation yielding steadier employment, but Nelson liked hard physical labour out of doors. Nor did the consequent financial uncertainties greatly mar the harmony of his domestic life. Admittedly, once or twice he had struck his wife in anger, coincidentally with one of the aforementioned sprees. But those were isolated, unrepresentative incidents. Speaking broadly, Nelson was a good father and a good husband.

On 4 September of that year Nelson had a spree. He made a day of it, from noon till almost midnight. In and out of hotels and bars and liquor stores. With buddies or alone. Vodka, brandy, beer, wine – enough to float a battleship; but Dale Nelson could carry it with the best. At the end, getting into his car, he felt fit enough to drive. And apparently he was. But he did not drive home. Although not far away.

He drove first to the house of Maureen McKay, a relative by marriage, separated from her husband, living alone with her four-year-old daughter. From there he drove two hundred yards to the house of Shirley Wasyk, another relative by marriage, living along with three daughters, (aged twelve, eight and seven) while her husband was away at a logging camp. From there he drove two miles further to the tiny farm of a man named Phipps, the last human dwelling before uninhabited wastes.

BELOW: Dale Nelson at the time of his arrest, 7 September 1970

At Mrs McKay's house, finding on reconnaissance that she had grown-up company, Nelson slunk away without even a knock or ring. At Mrs Wasyk's, he battered her to death and strangled the seven-year-old daughter; the twelve-year-old and the eight-year-old escaped. Do you inhale the faint scent of a bitter family feud? If so, mistakenly. Nelson had no relatives out at the Phipps farm, had had virtually no dealings with the farmer or his woman or their children (aged from ten years to eighteen months). Nonetheless, with rifle, club or knife, he killed them all. Eight people murdered within an hour or so. And still the worst is to be told of his iniquities.

In addition to the murders named, he ripped open the seven-year-old Wasyk girl from chest to groin, thrust his mouth into her stomach and ate undigested food; then, having made off with her body into the wastes, dismembered it, hiding somewhere the heart and genitals. He subjected the eight-year-old Wasyk girl to cunnilingus, and he abducted from the Phipps farm another eight-year-old girl, dead or dying, and (in the wastes) subjected her to buggery.

The Crown drew the inference – difficult to refute – that Nelson's real objective was possession of the young girls, and that murder of the rest was only incidental. The removal of obstacles to the gratification of his appetites. This inference gains extra credibility from an event which stands out as extraordinary even among so many extraordinary events. Nelson had not removed the seven-year-old's body on his first exit from the Wasyk house. He had run out precipitately on hearing the siren of police cars summoned by an unharmed but apprehensive Mrs McKay. Later, though, when the police had temporarily dispersed to evacuate other homesteads and scour environs, with infinite audacity he crept back inside, snatched the child's body, and drove on to the Phipps farm with his mutilated prize. Thus, in due course, he was able to head into the wastes with *two* young girls at his disposal for renewed atrocity.

Accepting the Crown's hypothesis concerning his objective, the vital question still awaited answer. What had occasioned this obscene explosion? Nelson had undoubtedly consumed a lot of alcohol, but not so as to prevent him controlling a car at speed along the unsurfaced tracks which zig-zagged through West Creston. Drunkenness, in any

159

event, was no defence to a murder charge or charges, unless it had made him incapable of forming the intent (when he might be convicted of manslaughter instead – followed, almost inevitably, by very long imprisonment). There was a hint, though no proof, of drugs, that he was 'smashed' on 'acid': 'Must have been the LSD' were almost the first words he spoke to his police captors, but he revoked them in a later statement (though past use by him of LSD was proved). It soon became apparent that the one defence promising succour was insanity.

This defence comprised four main constituents. 'Crazy' remarks uttered by Nelson during the aftermath: 'I had no reason to do anything. It seemed like it wasn't me.' 'Hallucinations' experienced by Nelson in his cell: mosquitoes, a large dog, Japanese girls on his bunk. (Holt, more than fifty years before, had complained of dogs and insects, but Japanese girls lay beyond the limits of his fancy.) A psychiatrist, of course: 'Schizo-affective psychosis. . . . A fluctuating condition. . . . Unable to appreciate that his actions in the Wasyk and Phipps homes were wrong.' (The Crown, of course, called psychiatrists in rebuttal.)

Much the most important constituent, however, much the strongest card that defence counsel had to play, was the

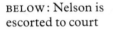

BELOW: Nelson is escorted to court

nightmarish narrative; the entirely undisputed record of the facts. No, the jury couldn't imagine themselves doing anything like it. But, yes, Nelson did know what he was doing. And yes, Nelson did know that it was wrong. The M'Naghten Rules directed them to a proper verdict.

The sub-human Nelson, though, did not forfeit his life. Bad ideas as well as good ideas are borrowed, and the Canadian Criminal Code had recently been amended to place different types of murder in different compartments (as did our own Homicide Act of 1957). The West Creston murders were not now capital. The Code fixed Nelson's penalty. Imprisonment for life. Sane or insane, he could not have hoped for anything better. His trial only settled *where* he was to be confined.

Leopold and Loeb were as wicked as Dale Nelson. Probably even wickeder. Indeed they would receive my personal nomination as the wickedest pair of murderers the world has ever known.

Nathan Leopold, aged nineteen, and Richard Loeb, aged eighteen, were cronies at Chicago University. Each came from a wealthy luxurious home; their fathers were reputed millionaires. Each had brains, each had charm; Loeb the more charm, Leopold the more brains. Each had devoted parents, numerous chums and girl friends. Each had *carte blanche* to make what he liked of his career. Who could ask for more?

Some who make excuses for them say they had too much. So that life was too easy. So that they got bored. Whether or no, late in 1923 – just when Capone was finding his feet in their home town – they conceived a notion of jointly carrying out a perfect murder. Perfect in that it could never be detected. Perfect in that they would never be accused. Perfect in that it would satisfy their egos that they were smarter than the forces of the law. Murder, not to avenge a wrong or annihilate an enemy. Murder for its own sake.

It was typical of them, and of their venture, that they chose their victim quite capriciously. On the appointed afternoon they sat in a hired car – for obvious reasons, they did not wish

ABOVE: Bobby Franks

to use one of their own – at a spot where they could watch the young sons of Chicago's rich coming out of their fashionable school.

If fourteen-year-old Bobby Franks had stayed in class or locker-room five minutes more – or less – odds on it would have been some other kid that was found next morning dead in a culvert in some prairie on Chicago's fringe. As it happened, they tempted Bobby – Loeb was his cousin – to get into the car with them, for a lift or ride. They killed him in the car, they got rid of the corpse as planned, without attracting any attention or suspicion. The perfect murder – if only Leopold's spectacles had not dropped from his pocket, so that they lay beside the culvert like a planted clue.

The detective work which followed was slow-moving but successful. From the spectacles to an optician, from the optician to Leopold, from Leopold to Loeb, from questions to confessions – only differing materially in that each blamed the other for the actual killing. *I* was driving, *he* bumped him off. *He* bumped him off, *I* was driving. Either way, it did not affect criminal liability. Either way, on their own stories, *both* of them were guilty.

One battle was over before it had begun; the battle to determine how Bobby Franks was killed. Another battle, though, was only just beginning: the battle to determine the sentence on his killers.

Their chief champion in that battle was America's most celebrated advocate, Clarence Darrow. The parents of Leopold and Loeb agreed to brief him; agreed to pay the staggering fee he asked; agreed to accept the unpalatable advice he gave. You must allow me to persuade the boys to let me plead them guilty. Then I can raise my voice for clemency, can argue that they were . . . you know, *non compos mentis*. That is the only chance of saving them from the rope. (The law provided a maximum punishment of death – and a minimum of fourteen years imprisonment.)

The strategy Darrow recommended being adopted, in issue was the mental condition of the accused. As in many a murder trial before and since. But the point was raised here in an unusual form. Darrow did not submit that his clients were Guilty but Insane, and therefore without legal responsibility *at all*. The question of mental state was only introduced as

162

affecting the *degree* of their responsibility, and, as a practical result, the degree of punishment. (The prosecution argued, without success, against its introduction into a plea of mitigation.)

ABOVE: Detectives aided by Richard Loeb (far right) search the ground at the spot where the body of Bobby Franks was discovered

The defence's psychiatrists (or alienists) led the way. 'Two maladjusted adolescents,' they reported, 'with a long background of abnormal mental life.' The state too, in its turn, produced psychiatrists. 'There is no evidence,' they reported,

163

'of mental disease.' Darrow did not display much faith in the psychiatrists. Not in the state's. Not even in his own.

I want to say to your honour that you may cut out every expert in this case, you may decide upon the facts alone, and there is no sort of question but what these boys were mentally diseased.

Mentally diseased – Darrow's interpretation of the phrase was wide. And as for discarding his experts, that was less bold a tactic than might appear. Remember – he did not set out to prove *insanity*, 'medical' or 'legal', only to present a general plea in mitigation, based primarily but not entirely upon state of mind. Even as to that, he made no pretence that his clients did not know what they were doing, or that they did not know what they were doing was wrong; he sought no protection under the M'Naghten Rules. To have done so would have required a full dress trial by jury. Darrow was perforce addressing himself to the judge. There were passages, though, redolent of his distinctive jury style; homespun, neighbour to neighbour over the wooden fence; the style that made him the Will Rogers of the Bar.

BELOW: Leopold and Loeb in court

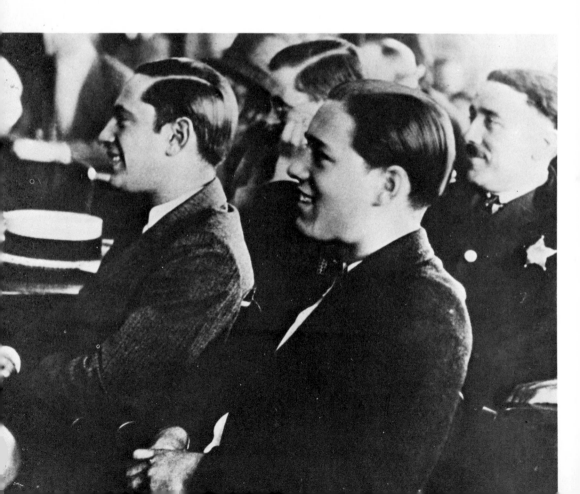

Now, your honor, you have been a boy. I have been a boy. We have known other boys. The best way to understand someone else is to put yourself in his place. Is it within the realm of your imagination that a boy who was right, with all the prospects of life before him, without the slightest reason in the world, would lure a young companion to his death, and take his place in the shadow of the gallows? ... There is not a sane thing in all of this from beginning to end.

The familiar question, in Darrow paraphrase. Can you imagine *anyone sane* doing anything like that? The question asked on behalf of Christie and Dale Nelson was asked on behalf of Leopold and Loeb.

In more flowery language, Darrow expatiated on the psychopathologies of his pampered clients. He called Loeb 'a child, wandering around in the morning of life, moved by the new feelings of the boy, moved by the uncontrolled impulses which his teaching was not strong enough to take care of, moved by the dreams and hallucinations which haunt the brain of a child.'

Teaching? Darrow made the same point more positively with Leopold, who had been a devotee of 'the dogmas taught by Nietzsche, with their cult of a hard and ruthless superman whose will overrides morality and virtue'. Appositely commenting that Nietzsche himself went mad, Darrow depicted Nathan Leopold as an American dupe of the European writer. 'A young boy, in the adolescent age, harassed by everything that harasses children, who takes this philosophy and believes it literally. It is a part of his life. It *is* his life.'

At some stage in his development of this theme, Darrow noticed something. That his honour was not, in their native parlance, overly impressed. The judge had said nothing to suggest that. He had not interrupted at all. To other observers he was totally impassive, conveying neither agreement nor dissent. But a great advocate must be a mind reader, not least in assessing the effect of his own words. It may have been the moment the judge chose to make a note, the tilt of his chin, an adjustment to his cuff. Or something even less determinate and tangible. But Darrow perceived that mental disease and Nietzsche, as items of extenuation, were not going down. That he must change his approach, discreetly shift his ground.

Had he detected a more encouraging reaction to his emphasis on 'boys', 'children', 'adolescents'? Possibly. Worth trying.

Many weeks had been spent devising and preparing the case for mental abnormality. More, though, was gained – if the outcome is a guide – by a few score words Darrow opportunely improvised.

If in this court a boy of eighteen and a boy of nineteen should be hanged on a plea of guilty, in violation of all the progress that has been made and of the humanity that has been shown in the care of the young, in violation of the law that places boys in reformatories instead of prisons – if your honour, in violation of all that and in face of all that, should stand here in Chicago to hang a boy on a plea of guilty, then we are turning our faces backwards towards the barbarism that once possessed the world.

Fallacies and fantasies abounded in Darrow's emotional and muddled rhetoric. Are persons of nineteen (or eighteen) justly grouped with children? Are children, as a general rule, haunted by hallucinations? Did care of the 'young' exclude young Bobby Franks? Did the murder of that little boy for fun denote much improvement on 'the barbarism that once possessed the world'? Much of Darrow's greatly admired speech was poppycock, and I should find it hard to believe that his honour did not think so. But for the advocate, the test was the result. And for the judge, it was *le dernier pas qui compte*.

He took several days for solitary reflection. On 10 September 1924, he pronounced sentence; charting the route by which he had reached it, step by step.

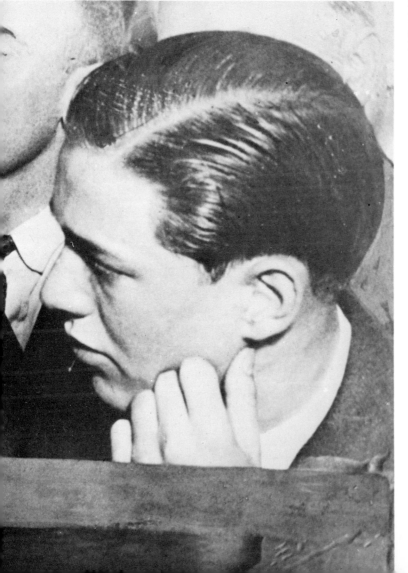

LEFT: Leopold and Loeb with their attorney, Clarence Darrow

The court is willing to recognize that the careful analysis of the life history of the defendants and of their present mental condition has been of extreme interest. . . . [But] the court is satisfied that [my] judgement in the present case . . . cannot be affected thereby.

So out of the window, with one heave, went the defence psychiatrists, Nietzsche, and Darrow's disquisitions on impulses and harassments. And with them the insanity thesis, gone beyond recall. Nothing to be allowed off punishment because of state of mind.

A crime of singular atrocity, it is, in a sense, inexplicable, but it is not thereby rendered less inhuman and repulsive. It was deliberately planned . . . during a considerable period of time. It was executed with every feature of callousness and cruelty. The crime is abhorrent to every instinct of humanity, and the court is satisfied that neither in the act itself, nor in its motives or lack of motives . . . can be found any mitigating circumstances.

So that had gone also, the hope that the murder's very pointlessness might have served to stave off condign retribution. In the prisoners' party, hearts that had sunk low sank lower still. Suddenly to rebound.

It would have been the path of least resistance to enforce the extreme penalty of the law. In choosing imprisonment instead of death, the court is moved chiefly by the consideration of the *age* of the defendants.

Cheers, tears, embraces. After all, they were not going to be hanged. For the moment it was almost as if they had been set free. Then the judge, continuing, injected cold reality. He passed on each defendant two separate sentences : for murder, confinement in the penitentiary for the rest of his natural life ; for kidnapping, confinement in the penitentiary for ninety-nine years. And, lest his intention was not absolutely clear, he strongly urged that they should never be paroled.

That recommendation was not ultimately observed. Loeb was killed in a prison brawl after eleven years. Leopold was released on licence after thirty-three. Better perhaps for law and Loeb and even Leopold if the judge had steeled himself, if they had both been hanged.

When insanity is pleaded as a defence, seldom does the upshot turn upon the cross-examination of one witness. And when it does, as at the trial of Ronald True, the witness is usually a mature man. Hardly ever, as at the trial of Harry Thaw, a young woman of surpassing beauty.

The plot of the Thaw case is too sensational, its characters too stock, for a novelist or a dramatist to risk. Evelyn Thaw, aged twenty-one, had been, as a teenage chorus girl, on terms of sexual intimacy with Stanford White. White, fifty-two, was America's foremost architect; also a lecher with a weakness for teenage girls. Harry Thaw, aged thirty-five, whom Evelyn had lately married was a spoilt playboy heir to railway millions, with a deserved name for violent temper and brutality.

On a June evening in 1906, all of them were at Madison Roof Gardens in New York for the opening of a show called 'Mam'zelle Champagne'. The Thaws and Stanford White,

RIGHT: Harry Thaw

however, were not together. Husband and wife were in a party, on the town for fun. White was alone, on the lookout for new talent. The newly-weds did not exchange greetings with the architect.

Early on Evelyn, bored by the performance or embarrassed by White's presence, got up to leave and was followed by her entourage. Save one. In the doorway, turning round, she asked: 'Where's Harry?'

Harry was standing behind and over Stanford White, holding a pistol pointed at his unsuspecting head. A moment later, a shot, then another, then another – once, twice, thrice, in the twinkling of an eye.

Evelyn went over. She saw attendants rushing to seize Harry Thaw. She saw the pool of blood spreading round White's body. 'I'll stick by you, Harry,' she said. Those are words to bear in mind. 'But, my God, you're in an awful mess.'

Had there not been, later, contrary indications, one would have guessed that Evelyn had a way of drawing it mild. Seldom, surely, was there a clearer act of murder committed before so many pairs of eyes. But Thaw's legal advisers conferred and cogitated until at last a defence of sorts evolved.

The interrelated parts of this defence were these. That Thaw had been born with what they called a psychopathic temperament – that is, he was not mad, but he was a man who, under heavy mental strain, might be driven *temporarily* mad. That when he first asked Evelyn to become his wife, she had refused, saying she was unworthy of that honour because, in her green youth and simple trustfulness, she had once been drugged and defiled by Stanford White. That, under pressure from Thaw – distraught with grief and rage – she had told him exactly what had happened: a deception which enticed her to White's studio, a glass of champagne, a pounding in her ears, a black-out, and a terrible awakening. That Thaw grew so obsessed with the wrong which had been done to this pure girl he loved, and with the wrongs that might have been done to others like her, he eventually worked himself into the delusion that Providence had chosen him to destroy the wrong-doer.

Far fetched? Undoubtedly. Hard to establish? Yes. But if they *could* establish it, Thaw was safely home. For the law of New York State relating to insanity and immunity was like that of Britain, like the M'Naghten Rules. And according to the picture drawn by the defence, while Thaw knew what he was doing when he killed Stanford White he did *not* know that it was wrong. He was convinced that it was right.

The composition of this picture at the trial would be shared. A delusion of divine command, a psychopathic temperament – these concepts could and must be put over by

BELOW LEFT: Evelyn Thaw shortly after her marriage

BELOW: Evelyn in later life

experts. But the deadly properties of the tale that triggered them off – these could be put over by Evelyn alone. Thaw's fate thus substantially depended on the impression that his wife made in court. On how moved and outraged the jury were by *her* recital of her tribulations. They would hardly believe that it had unhinged *him* if *they* could listen to it apathetically.

A huge burden to place upon slight shoulders. But Harry Thaw's advisers had inspected Evelyn – the great eyes, deep deep blue and soft as velvet; the mass of coiling, gleaming, long dark hair; the slender figure; the gentle, tranquil mouth. They had decided on the clothes she was to wear: simple dark blue frock, simple broad white collar, so that she looked hardly grown up, more like a lovely child. They were brimful of confidence when she took the stand.

Confidence which, for a while, seemed amply justified. Eyelids modestly lowered, voice softly pitched, she completely captivated that jury of males. As she narrated her injuries and woes a wave of anger and of pity swept across them. Such an innocent beauty, and such a vicious beast – it was beyond thought, it was beyond bearing. At the most poignant moments, they were near to tears. To learn that such a thing had happened to this child he worshipped – no wonder if it had pushed Harry Thaw over the edge.

The image of the innocent child, though, was badly stained when the District Attorney cross-examined.

He began by producing a single sheet of paper. Handing it to her. Watching her delicately moulded face.

'Did you write that letter?'

'Yes. I think so. Yes.'

'Is it addressed to the Mercantile Trust Company?'

'Er . . . yes. Yes.'

'Does it relate to a weekly sum of twenty-five dollars paid to you, through that company, by Stanford White?'

'Yes.'

'Being paid to you in 1902?'

'Yes.'

'Months before this drugging episode you have described?'

'Yes.'

'And you were accepting it?'

Evelyn puckered. Made no other answer. The artificial

dyke, though, had been broken. Came the flood.

Confessions poured out by the dozen, by the score. Yes, she had seen Stanford White, regularly, frequently, almost every day – *after* the date he had so wickedly betrayed her. Yes, she had visited him at the very studio. Yes, sometimes 'improprieties' had taken place. Yes, she had been co-respondent in two divorce suits. And so on and so forth. Up to the climax. *Before* her marriage, more than two years before, she had gone to bed at his apartment with the man so convinced of her saintlike purity that mere report of its pollution could unseat his reason. Yes, she had slept, unsanctified, with Harry Thaw.

The rest may pass unrecorded, may it not? You know without being told, the consequences of Evelyn's exposure; both as a girl who traded in her physical attractions, and as a player willing and able to perform a part. Guileless vestal into disingenuous harlot, demented Galahad into designing rake, safe asylum into execution shed. You think details would be superfluous?

Not at all.

The jury could not agree on a verdict. Seven for guilty, five for insane. So another trial. The whole routine, from start to finish. As a theatre includes a piece in repertory.

And the second jury? They did at least agree. Agreed that Harry Thaw was not responsible for that cold-blooded murder. Because – they were unanimous – at the time he was insane.

How mad is mad? I ask not about the accused, but about the juries.

It will be remarked that every one of the foregoing pleas was raised by the defendant to a charge of murder, at a place and time when capital punishment obtained. That is neither accidental nor tendentious; the scope for selection does not extend beyond. An insanity plea is virtually never made in cases other than murder, nor in murder cases if a death sentence is excluded. Indefinite detention in Broadmoor or an equivalent does not open up a prospect more agreeable than a finite term of detention in a jail (whether fixed, or masquerading as 'imprisonment for life'). It is, though, a tempting alternative to the gallows or the chair.

6.

SEX CRIMES

Alfred Whiteway
Edward Paisnel
Peter Griffiths
Patrick Byrne
Albert DeSalvo
Fritz Haarmann
Gaston Dominici

It would have had its own logic to start with crimes of sex, as without sex, there would not be any crimes at all. No sex, no procreation; no procreation, no people (the sole reliable recipe, that, for eradicating crime). No people, no criminals; no policemen to catch them; no courts to try them; no jailers to detain them; no probation and welfare officers to regenerate them. And so *ad infinitum*.

The human race came about, and survives, through 'normal' sex. The adjective is expressive, although misapplied. Sex is an urge, an impulse, like writing books (or reading them), and there are as many sexual as literary variations. The *average* sexual man (or woman) simply does not exist, any more than the average writer (or the average reader). 'Kinky?' said a prostitute, when someone used the word. 'If it means what I think it does, I've never had a client that wasn't.'

By definition, sex *crimes* are abnormal. In the legal sense. Not all – for example, sodomy – are deemed abnormal by opinion, and a sex crime, on analysis, may prove to be nothing but a 'normal' instinct carried to an unacceptable extreme.

The prime example of such a crime is rape.

Alfred Charles Whiteway, the Towpath Murderer of 1953, was a persistent, omnivorous, insatiable rapist. That was the way – the only way – he really enjoyed sex. He was not deprived of access to acquiescing women. He had an eighteen-year-old wife (he himself was twenty-two) who had borne him one child and was carrying another. If he craved for change, or the stimulus of licence, he did not even have to travel up to the West End; there were plenty of cheap prostitutes available in Kingston. But he was satisfied neither with marital nor hired intercourse, nor with an easy going girl-friend acquired by seduction. It was rape, with its preliminary excitement and its intrinsic violence, which – in the modern vernacular – turned him on.

Whiteway – what the Labour Exchanges call a construction worker, and who are known among themselves as brickies – was a lout. Shovelling muck around on a building site, or, with prophetic symbolism, clambering up a scaffold. He attended to this work, however, only when he felt like it. More often he felt like cycling round the countryside, wearing a leather jacket and a high-necked vest, crepe soles on his shoes and a small axe in his saddlebag, deliberately hunting for females he could rape. The bicycle gave him a wide choice of localities: from Oxshott to Chislehurst, from Windsor Great Park to Ruislip. Crude sharp lust gave him a wide choice of victims: a child of twelve, a matron of fifty-six – each potential grist for the mill, as long as unaccompanied. The axe – in use, or as a threat – gave him wide success; like some men chalk up conquests, he chalked up violations. These outrages, separated more by space than time, totalled rapidly six, eight, ten, a dozen. To the police they presented an unfolding pattern, consistent in design, details – and, above all, *brutality*. They were one man's doing. One man – who would be popularly termed a 'sex maniac'. One man – who roamed lanes and woods like a savage beast of prey. One man – of that they were more sure with each successive incident, but they had no clue, no lead as to who he was. Until a Sunday at the very end of May.

That weekend three youths had been camping in a field alongside the towpath of the Thames at Teddington. On the Sunday, at about 8 pm, they were joined by two young girls of their acquaintance. The evening was spent in typical juvenile

BELOW: The victims of the Towpath Murderer, Christine Reed and Barbara Songhurst

horse play: chaffing, chasing, hide and seek among the bushes, with harmless overtones like a snatched kiss or a squeeze. About 11 pm the girls got on their bicycles and rode back together along the towpath. The youths waved to them until they had both vanished into the dark.

Neither reached home. Subsequently their corpses were recovered from the river. Heads battered, bodies stabbed – and raped.

'The sexual assault,' reported the examining pathologist, 'was of the most violent type. Before the assault, both were *virgo intacta*.' The second fact betokens the virtue of the girls, the first the sexual potency of their assailant. Because – it is obvious from the circumstances – the rapes must have followed each other almost without an interval.

'I'm mental,' Whiteway declared in his statement to the police. 'Me head must be wrong. I cannot stop meself.' That seemed to foreshadow, even pave the way for, a defence, but no plea of insanity was entered at his trial. He was a 'sex maniac', but he was not mad. He relied on a blanket denial – 'I

RIGHT: Whiteway at the time of his arrest, September 1953

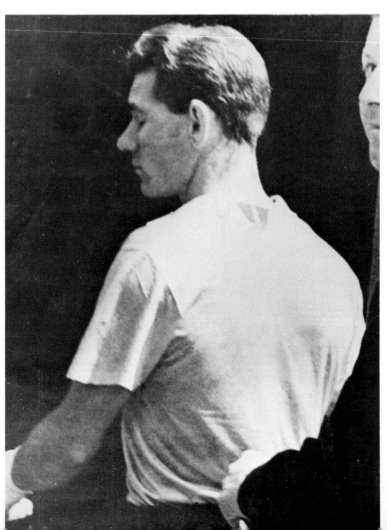

did nothing, I know nothing' – plus an alibi which crumbled at a touch. The evidence (including a signed confession which he repudiated: 'I didn't look at what I was signing, I was shown where to sign') satisfied the jury that he *was* the Towpath Murderer (the events elsewhere, of course, were never mentioned), and on 22 December Whiteway hanged.

Just as well. The idiosyncratic series of attacks naturally ceased from the hour of his arrest. But if he had committed the murders twelve years later, after capital punishment in Britain was ended, he would now doubtless be out of jail again (braced to face the world by a reformative regime of visits from Lord Longford). This very day he could be back in the old routine: leather jacket, crepe shoes, small axe in the saddlebag.

Oxshott. Chislehurst. Windsor Great Park. Ruislip. Teddington.

Whiteway was mentally undeveloped and unsubtle; Edward Paisnel – just as hateful – was a remarkable man. He kept the countrydwellers on the Channel Island of Jersey under a reign of terror for *more than fifteen years*; he took youngsters from their beds in lonely but inhabited houses, and then subjected them to unspeakable obscenities; he wore on these nocturnal expeditions grotesque garb and a terrifying mask; he kept those accoutrements, when not required, in a secret room; he dabbled – if no more – in black magic and Satanism, collecting dubious books and chalices and relics; he maintained all the while the image of a respectable citizen – a self-employed contractor and jobbing gardener.

And, incidental to these things – he confirmed one strongly held belief and upset another. The former – that a full moon stimulates weird behaviour. The latter – that robbers (whether looking for cash or jewels or children) steer clear of a house where adults are at home.

The domiciliary raids began in 1957. Thereafter they recurred sporadically; sometimes in swift bursts, once after an uninterrupted break of three whole years. The total sum of Paisnel's crimes defies exact enumeration, but twenty – the moderate police estimate – will serve.

A Paisnel operation passed, usually, through six stages. First, patiently casing the joint until he was familiar with

ABOVE: Edward Paisnel, September 1971

windows and doors and juxtaposition of the rooms. Second, entry and abduction, effected by threat or force or fraud ('Don't shout or I'll kill you'; 'My knife is sharp'; 'I have a gun'). Third, expertly blindfolding the abductee as re-insurance of the protection afforded by his mask. Fourth, leading or dragging the victim to a neighbouring field. Fifth, an act of rape – or sodomy – with a girl, an act of sodomy – or fellatio – with a boy. Sixth, at high risk, escorting his coerced sexual partner back to the house, back to the room, back even to bed. Solicitous, tender almost – but the jobbing gardener was always nice with children.

Two of Paisnel's most audacious enterprises demonstrate how the system worked in actual practice.

A boy – a boy of nine. Innocent, truthful, rather babyish for his age. Peacefully sleeping, barely a yard from his small brother. Wakened by a torch flashing into his eyes.

'Come on,' says a muffled voice. 'Come on.'

The boy peers unavailingly into the bright light. Is it Daddy? Surely no; Daddy and Mummy have kissed him goodnight, and gone into their bedroom. Anyway, Daddy wouldn't play a joke like this. At *this* time. Who then?

'Come on. Come on.'

The boy can glimpse the stranger now. A funny-looking person! *Terribly* funny. Puffy cheeks. Flabby lips. Dirty, straggly hair. Nasty-like. Afterwards the boy speaks of him as the Bogey Man.

'Come on.'

'Where? What for?'

'Sssh. Quiet, now. Or I'll cut your throat. See?'

The boy sees – sees a penknife in the stranger's hand. Ordered to get up, he does. Half dazed, half afraid. His small brother, in the other bed, sleeps on.

'Piggyback?' suggests the stranger, in a whisper.

Yes, the boy likes piggybacks. It works like the classical bait of sweets. Carrying him, the stranger tiptoes softly down the stairs.

There are french windows at the back. They go through, down the garden, across some waste ground. The boy is no longer dazed, but much more afraid.

'Drop them,' says the stranger.

'Drop what?' says the boy.

A rough hand feels inside the gap in his pyjamas. . . .

A girl – a girl of fourteen. Living with her widowed mother. In a cottage; modern, spruce, comfortable, but secluded. Stirring in her beauty sleep. Hearing a knock and noises in the hall below. Wondering if she is dreaming. Then a loud shout. Calling her by name.

'Stay in your room and lock the door.'

Her mother's voice. No dream. No doubt. No possible mistake. Her mother's voice – but in a tone she has never heard before. Stricken with terror. Quivering with alarm.

The girl leaps up. As she opens her bedroom door, the front door slams.

'Mother . . . Mother. . . .'

Only an empty soundlessness. As though the cottage also holds its breath. Wondering, the girl goes down the stairs.

'Mother . . . Mother. . . .'

But Mother is hastening to the nearest house for help.

From somewhere a rough hand reaches out of the darkness. A hard punch fells the girl. A rope is tied around her neck.

'Come on.'

As she resists and pulls away, automatically she tightens the rope until she nearly chokes.

'Come on.'

She has no option. Barefoot, led as by a halter, she advances with her captor into the open air.

'I've killed before, and I'm ready to kill again. Drop them. And lie down.'

The girl – who blames her? – chooses a fate marginally better than death. . . . .

On a smaller ration, Macbeth felt he had 'supt full with horrors'. But much worse than Whiteway and Paisnel (jailed for thirty years) is to come, and cannot, without dodging reality, be skated over. The cases of Peter Griffiths and Patrick Byrne

If he had not been followed by Byrne just over ten years later, Griffiths, who made the country blench in 1948, would still be without any rival amongst rapist monsters. As it is, the pair may wrestle in perdition for priority.

A hospital. Near Blackburn, Lancashire. The Babies' Ward, on 14 May, at night. Of the cots with high rails lined up along each wall, six had tiny occupants; the oldest, June Devaney, was not yet four. A lively child, the only inmate who could talk, she had been brought in with a chest complaint. Recovered, she was due for discharge the next day. When the night nurse came on duty at 11.30, she made the customary round of all her charges. June was sleeping soundly.

For the next hour or so, the nurse's duties took her to and fro – in and out of the kitchen and the Toddlers' Ward nearby. She also paid several further visits to the Babies'

OPPOSITE: The grotesque disguise used by Paisnel to terrorize the people of Jersey for more than ten years

DAILY EXPRESS

No. 22,220   FRIDAY NOVEMBER 26 1971   Weather: Sunny spells; mainly dry   Price 3p

THE VOICE OF BRITAIN

Cheers for Sir Alec

HOME THE HERO

By
WALTER PARTINGTON

IT was to a hero's welcome, voiced in a solid and deafening Tory roar, that Sir Alec Douglas-Home rose in the Commons yesterday to announce the historic Rhodesian peace deal.

The 68-year-old Foreign Secretary was visibly tired at the end of nine days of hard bargaining and a 17-hour night flight home as he spelled out the "fair and honourable" settlement terms.

These will give Rhodesia's Africans more votes, more land, and more rights.

If the deal is accepted "by the people as a whole"—Lord Pearce, chairman of the Press Council and a former law lord, will head a commission to "test" that acceptability—it will end the six-year-old independence dispute. Sir Alec said the proposals were "fully within the five principles to which the Government have constantly adhered."

HARMONY

Quote

Their president, he declared, an opportunity to set a new course in Rhodesia which can lead to greater harmony of all races there and to the partnership and prosperity of all Rhodesians.

He warned the House: Let us be in no doubt that the price that will be paid if we fail in this attempt will be paid not by us but by others—meaning Rhodesia's Africans.

Mr Alec faced Labour yells of "Sell out" and "Give him an umbrella"—a reference to his visit to Rhodes in 1938 with Mr Neville Chamberlain—with unruffled calm.

There were taunts from Mr. Andrew Faulds (Lab. Smethwick) that the settlement marked "a shameful day" and from Mr. Denis Healey, Shadow Foreign Secretary, who caused uproar when he referred to Mr. Alec's "record of gullibility in 1938."

Mr. Healey did say: "Anyone who listened to the Foreign Secretary will recognise that the North rejoice appears to have made some concessions."

But he said the House would want answers to some questions—in particular, would there be effective protection against violation of the agreement after sanctions had been removed.

Mr. Gilbert Longden (Tory, Herts S.W.) urged the Opposition to be generous. He said the agreement for Mr Alec had "brought back a sense of the national honour and pride."

ULSTER: WILSON SURPRISE

By WILFRID SENDALL and ROY BLACKMAN

A PLAN for a United Ireland within the Commonwealth was put to the Government by Mr. Wilson last night.

It would be moulded on Britain, using her legal, education, and social systems.

And it would be debated on Britain, using her legal, education, and social systems.

The Labour leader, opening the Commons debate on Ulster after his visit there, saw his plan as the only long-term solution.

BUT there could be NO withdrawal of British troops. That would rule "criminal madness and murderous," he said.

QUEEN

He proposed a permanent Army garrison throughout its 15 years—and five or 10 years longer if the Governments of a United Ireland was to.

THE PROJECT would start with talks between the three Governments—Westminster, Stormont and Dublin—who would appoint an all-party commission to decide the Constitution of the new Ireland.

After agreement, Eire would seek Commonwealth membership, recognising the Queen as head. Ulster would then transition away from a political weapon.

The new Constitution would take effect after the 10-year transition period provided that citizens as a political weapon has been.

Home Secretary Mr. Maudling is expected to reply to the proposals when he speaks in the debate tonight.

REACTION LAST NIGHT :
Ulster Premier Brian Faulkner : "Cloud cuckooland talk." He saw no prospect of linking with Eire "as far as the Eire Premier Jack Lynch : "A serious contribution to finding a way forward."

● Meanwhile Mr. Wilson's policy came under fire at a private meeting of Labour MPs who insisted on forcing a vote against the Government when the debate ends on Monday.

Seven tell 'How we escaped'

Seven of the nine men who escaped from Belfast's Crumlin Road jail on November 16 appeared at a Press conference in Dublin yesterday.

They said they got over the wall with rope ladders flung from outside and arrived in Dublin almost a week ago.

Smith: Our future

JOHN MONKS

SALISBURY, Thursday.

PREMIER Ian Smith today told Rhodesians he had agreed to settle with Britain.

He could have gone on in we are now," he said in a Parliamentary statement. "From rags to the country. "But in 16 or 20 years' time the position would not have been so good for our children."

Hundreds of Africans sat in the inner's bureau outside Parliament to hear Mr. Smith's speech relayed through loudspeakers.

He said a settlement had been reached because of "give" and take on both sides."

Speaking on the key section of the agreement which provides for unimpeded progress to majority rule, he told worried Rhodesians that it would be a realistic position to try and resist when Africans obtained the majority in the country in Rhodesia.

TROUBLE AT UNO

NEW YORK, Thursday.

RUSSIA bitterly denounced the Rhodesian settlement terms in the United Nations Security Council today.

Russian Ambassador Jacob Malik described it as "a bargain between an English lord and a Southern Rhodesian racist."

The council meeting is considering whether a settlement with Rhodesia and "no guarantees" that majority harbour any anxiety as to his future in Rhodesia.

Sex case sensation

Mask, wig, and nails: a dummy dressed up as an alleged child-attacker

COURT SEES THIS MASK AND COAT OF NAILS

By ALFRED DRAPER

HERE on the left, an outfit shown to a court at the rear of a sex attacker.

A grotesque rubber mask, a shaggy wig, and a coat and a pair of wrist gloves with nails sticking out.

This is how a former father of three, Edward Pinset, is alleged to have

dressed up to assault two girls and two boys.

The picture, of a dummy, was released by the Royal Court of Jersey.

Yesterday Pinset wore handcuffs and a coat over his head. That was when, with members of the court, he was taken lower for an inspection of the "secret room" with its "cellar" and witchcraft books.

Back in court it was announced that Pinset, who pleads not guilty, would not give evidence.

His father and girl friend said he was with them when alleged to have committed sex assaults.

The case goes on today.

LATEST

TV-Radio programmes Page 17

FORGED FIVERS
(See this paper)

Scotland Yard customs experts flying an Amsterdam letter or tomorrow to help with inquiries on forged fivers case.

PHONE STD CODE 01

353 8000

TELEX 21841

'Top money talks'

By OSBERT LANCASTER

BONN, Thursday.—A By-Post meeting between President Brandt, Mr Heath, Chancellor Brandt and President Pompidou is being discussed. West German sources say.

The Summit, to examine monetary problems, could be during President Nixon's visit to the Azores on December 13 to see President Pompidou.

Dud fivers : Five held

THREE Britons and two South Africans are being held in Holland following a Scotland Yard investigation into a flood of forged £5 notes found to have surged into the London area.

The South Africans were arrested as they were being flown home from Heathrow.

The T.d. Congress had voted to end sanctions against the importation of high-grade Rhodesian tobacco.

Prison riot

NEW YORK, Thursday.

About 1,000 inmates of Rahway State Prison, New Jersey, are holding the warden and the guards hostage today after a riot over conditions. Officials have refused to negotiate.

TV blackout

FIVE million television screens were blacked out last night when Southern transmitter stopped transmitting because of an unknown key dispute.

What a match!

TV star Warne Reid
is to marry Wexford Times top Eileen Keith Worthington after a secret romance. Warne, 34, and Eileen, 33, announced their engagement yesterday.

Rolls ultimatum

The Rolls-Royce motor factory at Crewe will close unless a work-to-rule ends, say bosses. The 7,000 workers were told yesterday.

21 too many

There have been so many complaints about men being given "a warning" by Lord Goodman who did so much work to get one of the key proposals, the Declaration of Rights, which will have been moving closer over the past five of us last years.

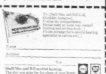

Ward. All was well. Until a quarter past one, when the nurse, glancing round, saw that June had vanished. That her cot was empty.

The nurse's first reaction was stunned astonishment. It was incredible – quite impossible – that the child could have climbed those high rails, got out of the cot herself. And who would wish to take her? Who would have the chance? What the nurse did not know then, but what transpired afterwards, was summarized by the judge for the jury at the trial.

Between a quarter past twelve and a quarter past one, the guilty person got into the ward, in the hospital, without any shoes on; how he got in does not matter – the point is, he did. He takes out of the bed this poor little child and walks out of the ward with her – probably you will think through the porch, or maybe through the window. He took this child in the middle of the night, up to the far end of that wall [a stone wall enclosing the grounds of the entire hospital], and, having raped her in the most dreadful circumstances, dashed her brains out against the wall.

Raped in the most dreadful circumstances? Even more dreadful than the victim's age, taken by itself, suggests? Let the doctor tell – the police surgeon who conducted the post-mortem.

BELOW: An aerial view of Queen's Park Hospital, Blackburn, showing the spot, marked 'A', where Griffiths broke into the hospital and the spot, marked 'B' where the body of June Devaney was found

There were extensive bruises over the whole of the face. . . . There was a multiple fracture of the skull. . . . Blood was exuding from the nose. . . . There were several punctured wounds on the left foot. They might easily have been caused by finger nails gripping the left ankle. . . . The injuries to the head were consistent with the head having been battered against a wall. [There was blood on the wall just above where June was found, nearly three hundred yards away from her cot in the Babies' Ward.] It appears to me that the child was *held by her feet and the head swung against the wall.*

Untrained, as well as trained, minds could draw the deduction. As prosecuting counsel said, 'The lust of some well-built man had sought to satisfy itself on the frail body of that child,' and had added to a most foul, strange and unnatural rape a most foul, ruthless and repugnant murder. Was the latter motiveless – a gratuitous encore by uninhibited barbarity? Quite possibly, but I think there is a likelier explanation. In nameless terror and agonizing pain, June must have screamed and shrieked with all her puny strength. The rapist would not be finicky in silencing her.

Never was the public more appalled by a crime. Never was the public more incensed by a criminal. Never did the police rise to a challenge more resourcefully. There were no inspired coups of a kind to vie with Sherlock Holmes. The tracking down of Griffiths was a triumph for *thoroughness*. As such, it has a permanent place in the history of detection.

Admittedly the police did start with a priceless bonus – the one that every detective prays for – fingerprints. Procured from a Winchester bottle, one of those large containers commonly used in hospitals, which, during the nurse's fateful and fatal absence, had been moved from a trolley to the floor beneath June's cot. There were several sets of impressions on the bottle. The fingerprints of hospital staff were taken and eliminated. An alien set remained. Those – it was almost certain – were the criminal's.

But fingerprints at the *locus in quo*, though potentially conclusive, can only get results upon comparison with others. A suspect's, for instance, or a set preserved in the fingerprint bureau of Scotland Yard. But there were no suspects. And none in the Bureau corresponded with the prints on the bottle – which meant that the rapist-murderer had no serious criminal record. The police persevered. They sent copies of

the bottle prints to every force in Britain. They sent copies to every fingerprint bureau in the world. They fingerprinted every male over sixteen in the town.

In that last process, 46,000 sets of prints were taken. Experts spent countless hours sifting them; studying them side by side with the Winchester bottle prints. At last – they checked again – at last a set that tallied. Those of Peter Griffiths: former Guardsman, of no present occupation, aged twenty-two, living with his parents. Other evidence now accumulated and fitted into place. Marks of stockinged feet on the ward's polished floor exactly matched Griffiths's stockinged footmarks. Woollen fibres found on June's body and her nightdress exactly matched those of Griffiths's one and only suit. Arrested, he made a statement in which he confessed. But none of this would have come to light or occurred without the fingerprints. Prosecuting counsel said: 'If there had been a less thorough combing he might have escaped.' Take it a step further. Say he *would* have done.

Peter Griffiths, on the surface, seemed nothing like the ogre his atrocities suggest. He was what is often called 'a clean-looking lad'; regular features, frank eyes, an air of being

186

freshly and scrupulously scrubbed. His family was poor but honest; his background colourless; his nature indolent. He had no men pals, and the only girl to whom he was attached had broken with him because, she said, he drank too much. But he was neither a sociable nor an anti-social drinker. He did not get aggressive or rough. He did not carouse with constant or casual companions. On the evening of the rape–murder he went out – I quote his words – 'to spend a quiet night alone'. Going from one pub to another, he had eleven pints of beer, two Guinnesses and two double rums. That, on his own count. That, between six o'clock and closing time.

Griffiths's statement may have been inaccurate in some minor details, but there is no reason to doubt that in essentials

LEFT: Peter Griffiths

it was true. The vital part begins with him leaving his shoes on the veranda outside the Babies' Ward.

I went in and I heard a nurse humming and banging things as if she was washing something so I came out again and waited. Then I went back in again and went straight in the ward. . . . I picked up a biggish bottle . . . went half way down the ward with it then put it down on the floor. . . . I picked the girl up out of the cot and took her outside by the same door. I carried her in my right arm and she put her arms around my neck and I walked with her down the hospital field. I put her down on the grass. . . . She wouldn't stop crying. I just lost my temper then and you know what happened then.

Indeed they knew, we all know but too well, what happened then.

At his trial, Griffiths did not retract that statement. He pleaded – formally – Not Guilty, but the facts were un-disputed, and he himself did not go into the box. Psychiatrists spoke instead – to say that he had schizophrenia; that, as a result, he had developed a maniacal frenzy; that, as a result, when he raped and murdered June Devaney, he did not know that what he was doing was wrong. Any credibility that this theory possessed was destroyed by three questions Mr Justice Oliver asked one of the psychiatric witnesses.

'You said, did you not, that the mania developed when he began attacking the child?'

'Yes.'

'At what stage did it cease?'

'After he killed the child.'

The boundaries of mania having been drawn, a little later:

'Why did he take her out of bed in the middle of the night and carry her into a field?'

The psychiatrist recognized the impasse.

'I have no idea,' he said.

Rounding off his statement with implied self-condemnation (Schizophrenic convulsion? Developing mania?) Griffiths had remarked: 'I hope I get what I deserve.'

He got it.

Byrne was a big drinker, too, but of the opposite kind. Not for him solitary, introspective, bouts. A rotund, jolly, Irish labourer of twenty-eight, with two chins and the shadow of a third, he rejoiced in noisy 'sessions' with his mates. Broad jokes interminably retold, large glasses interminably refilled. No girls; Byrne had no time, socially, for girls. His was a love-hate attitude towards the female sex; obsessed by Woman, terrified of women. That he was an erotic fantasist was probable. That he was a peeping Tom is certain. After dark, an accessible lighted window drew him like a magnet; if lucky, he could feast his eyes on a pretty girl, undressing or undressed. Feast his eyes – and nothing more. Like the patrons of a strip-tease, he thus got sexual thrills without approach or contact, without effort or obligation. So long as this reprehensible but relatively innocuous relief and re-creation contented him, so good.

In December 1959, during the run-up to Christmas, Byrne had been employed at Birmingham, on a building site. On the 23rd, about 1 pm, Byrne ('with Paddy Duff, two Scotch chaps, and another Irishman') went to an adjacent pub. What happened may best be conveyed in his own words.

We had a drinking session there, leaving just before three o'clock, and then we all went to the site. All of us went to the hut and there was some card playing and a lot of shouting and bawling. . . . The foreman came in and swept us all out. . . . I hung about until everybody finished work then I got my cards and money. I put Duffy on his bus about quarter to five and then went dilly-dallying on my way home walking all the time and I remember finishing up in Wheeleys Road near the YWCA. . . . I knew the hostel there because I don't live far away.

A drive led up to the hostel from the road. Byrne walked along it, staring at the windows.

'Some of them were alight. . . . I thought I would like to have a peep through a window. I have done this before a few times.'

The only lighted window within reach had a curtain drawn across. But not completely. Byrne peered through the chink. A girl, in a jumper and underskirt. Combing her hair.

Stephanie Baird worked in an office. She was twenty-nine. Modest, rather shy, she kept herself to herself, especially with regard to men. No boy-friends – though not for want of aspirants. For Stephanie was attractive, even beautiful. Had she not been so, she might still have been alive.

Some sex criminals are indifferent to sex-appeal. Byrne, though, was choosy. He fancied Stephanie. He climbed through another window into the corridor and stood on a chair looking through the glass over her door.

I was just going to go when she opened the door. She came face to face with me and asked what I was doing. . . . We were standing quite close together then and I was just going to run and as I turned my arm touched her breasts. This got me excited and I got hold of her breast. I said 'Give me a kiss' and before she could say no I kissed her. She tried to shove me away but couldn't. . . . I was feeling her all over and kissing her but she screamed and then I put my hands round her neck.

190

It is astonishing that nobody heard the ensuing commotion. As she was being strangled, Stephanie fell backwards; her head, said Byrne, 'bounced' on the floor – her skull was fractured. He lay on top of her 'kissing and squeezing her neck at the one time'. It may be assumed – and must be hoped – that she died almost at once. Byrne 'felt sure' she was dead before he turned to sex.

'I bolted the door. I took my trousers and my jacket and my shirt off and I was naked apart from my shoes and socks. I rolled all over her. Her underclothes were all round her waist.'

Sated, or spent, Byrne 'got tired of that'. Already he had done enough to assure his name a singularity among sex criminals. But now, in an open cupboard, he spotted a knife. An ordinary table knife. Domestic cutlery. It revived malign desires. In yet more macabre form.

'I got the knife in my right hand then and caught hold of her right breast and carved the knife round it. . . . I was very surprised and disappointed it came away flat in my hand. I just looked at it and flung it towards the bed. I scored round her chest with a knife.'

Mammary mutilation, however horrible, has obvious – distorted – roots in sex. Byrne's crowning outrage, though, seems to have roots only in horror.

'I started on the back of the neck then. . . . I kept on cutting away. . . . When the head came off I had it by the hair and I stood up. I held it up to the mirror and looked at it through the mirror.'

Why? Seven weeks later, run to earth, Byrne said he did not know. 'It's been puzzling me since why I cut off the head.' Whatever may have been his baffling and consuming fire, even that dreadful deed did not extinguish it. He had had the urge to kill – and the audacity to attack – another girl in the hostel before he finally fled. For this he did offer what may pass as explanation. 'I was thinking that I ought to terrorize all the women. I wanted to get my own back on them for causing my nervous tension through sex.'

Not even a tame psychiatrist to submit Byrne was insane. Instead he pleaded 'diminished responsibility' under the Homicide Act of 1957. A sensible jury nonetheless convicted him of murder. Preserved from the gallows by the same

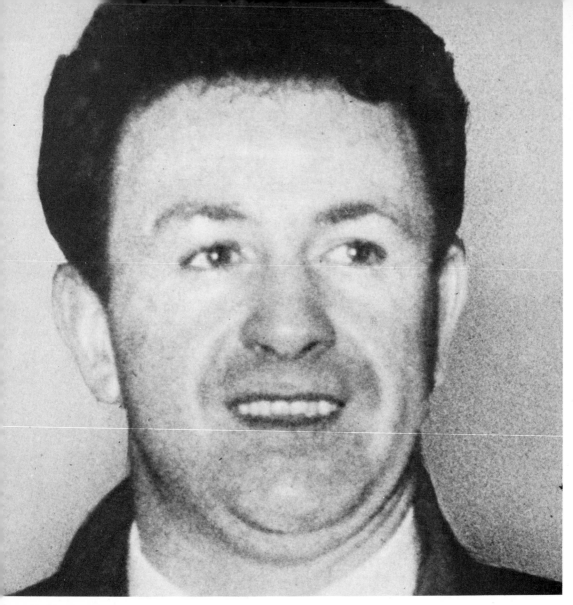

ABOVE: Patrick Byrne at the time of his arrest

fatuous Act, he was sentenced, 'as prescribed', to life imprisonment.

It was not till the trial of Christie in 1953 that necrophily, as word or as idea, came within the boundaries of English public knowledge. Byrne also would appear to have been a necrophile – allowing the expression some flexibility. He did have sex with a woman dead or dying, but her condition was not essential to his sexual 'kicks'. He did not want sex with her because she was dead or dying; she was dead or dying because he wanted sex. So Byrne does not, in this respect, resemble Christie. A closer parallel is with the Boston Strangler.

Like Jack the Ripper with the whores of Whitechapel during the autumn of 1888, the Boston Strangler created an empire of suspense and fear. But over a longer period, a wider area, and with an entirely different sort of woman.

The Strangler's dominion lasted eighteen months – from June 1962 to January 1964. It covered not only Boston – Back Bay, Beacon Hill – but points on the periphery: Cambridge, Salem, Lynn. His prey were not prostitutes, either cheap or costly; varying in social or economic status, they were all what are called 'straight' girls by prostitutes themselves. Girls, perhaps, is a misnomer, for the Strangler took high toll of the elderly; his first five victims were, in order, aged fifty-five, fifty-seven, sixty-eight, seventy-five, sixty-seven. Those that came later tended to be younger: twenty-three, twenty, even nineteen. One of the very last in line, however, was fifty-six. The grand total cannot be determined – least of all from his own subsequent account. Sex criminals are selective in their reminiscences. But it was certainly not less than a dozen.

Like Byrne, he murdered to get sex, either by 'normal' copulatory penetration, or by 'playing around' (his own informative expression), or by 'the insertion of a foreign body'. When he did these things, he sometimes knew that the woman was aware; sometimes that she was unconscious; sometimes that she was dead. Sometimes he simply did not know one way or another – and does not seem to have cared.

His campaign had a terrible simplicity, the separate engagements an artistic uniformity. A call at the entrance of a large apartment block. A quick inspection of the plates beside the buzzers. A marking down of one flat – otherwise at random – which happened to be labled with a woman's name. An assurance – gained by oblique enquiry – that the female occupant was there quite on her own. An entry obtained by plausible excuse; 'I'm from the landlord, come to inspect ceilings, windows, pipes. A tour ostensibly searching for leaks, cracks, draughts. A blow on the head or an arm round the neck when her back was turned. Stripping off – her always, himself occasionally. After sex, the body posed suggestively and lewdly, the breasts tilting upwards, the bare legs straddling wide.

The Strangler – Albert DeSalvo. How do we know *who* he was? Because in the end, still undetected, he owned up. But only after he had partially paid for a mistake – or, on a charitable view, an unwonted act of mercy.

In October 1964 DeSalvo committed a rape which was not combined with murder. The woman was able to give the police his full description. It corresponded with that of a man they had in the past had tabs on. A man who had worked with immunity a minor sexual con trick – persuading women to let him 'measure' them, bust and thigh, on the pretext that he was recruiting 'models'. This man, brought in, was identified by the woman who had been raped – and spared. Before the judge he behaved so strangely that he was committed, until further order, to a State mental hospital. While there, he confessed to being the Strangler – on condition that his confession would not be used against him. But the police could confirm that what he said was true from the multitude of details he supplied. Nature of injuries, colour of bras, décor, furniture. Details never disclosed to the press and public. Details which only the Strangler could have known.

BELOW: Albert De-Salvo is taken into custody after his escape from the mental hospital where he had been detained, 25 February 1967

The Strangler – what sort of an individual was DeSalvo? In his mid-thirties, medium height, athletically built, with hands which were too large and eyes which were too small. He was a casual labourer with a 'record' – but only of petty crimes, mostly breaking and entering; never a charge, still less a conviction, for any sex offence. 'A good provider and family man', he was fond of his two small children; he complained, though, that his wife was 'cold' and often refused him intercourse – a serious matter because DeSalvo was plainly oversexed ('Five or six times a day don't mean much to me').

The Strangler – why did he do it? Many will say, no need to ask. But randy husbands and frigid wives are neither new nor rare, and extra-marital sex does not postulate rape and murder. DeSalvo has given, for what it is worth, a personal explanation. 'I'm driving to work and I'm building the image up and then I get release right in my underwear but five minutes later I'm ready again and the image comes back and the pressure mounts in my head, you understand me?'

I for one understand him perfectly. He is pleading what psychiatrists call an irresistible impulse. What less fanciful folk call an impulse unresisted. Mrs DeSalvo hit the nail upon the head, remonstrating with her tiresomely tumescent spouse. 'Al, you can learn by yourself to control yourself. It is just a matter of self-control.'

The legislation epitomized by the phrase 'consenting adults' – as sensible as the Homicide Act was senseless – brought the English law into line with civilized opinion. Formerly punishable by life imprisonment, sex in private between males is now no longer a crime at all – unless involving force or corrupting youth. Thus acknowledging, far in the wake of Periclean Athens, that homosexuality is not culpable in itself, but only when indulged in a form injurious to society. A sign of rational moral thought, unusual in our age.

Neither rational thinking nor the most liberal laws, though, could possibly have found extenuation for Fritz Haarmann. Before being beheaded (for murder at his native Hanover in 1925) he *had* corrupted the relatively young in massive numbers – with extraneous subsequent embellishments never practised by the predators of Playland. After using boys sexually, he killed and ate them, or, at very least, sold them to be eaten. The two transactions were connected only for convenience; Haarmann was less a cannibalistic homosexual than a homosexual who was also cannibalistic. His cannibalism was more unnatural than his homosexuality. His homosexuality is more representative. A perfect specimen of a 'queer'; perfectly set in time and place.

Modern Germany has been the world's shop window for perversion. Post-war periods are notorious for degeneracy. Haarmann was a German of the lower middle class who reached forty in the first year after the First World War (which he spent in a civil jail for a string of thefts). Economic and social institutions were dissolving – to produce the collapse of the Mark and the emergence of the Nazis; to foster and facilitate the vile career of Haarmann. 'His,' said William Bolitho, 'is the sum of all their guilt [referring to mass murderers]. . . . This man was the *chief* murderer, the *worst* man, the *last of the human race*.' The italics are mine, but not the unique condemnation; in thus singling out Haarmann among devils, it goes too far. Only just too far, however. Judge from the facts.

At that time Hanover roughly compared in size with Bristol, Stockholm, Edinburgh, Toronto. A population of somewhere about four hundred thousand. An historic name and a geographical position which made it a naturally centripetal metropolis, a Mecca of the discontented for miles around. And especially the discontented young. Boys whose fathers had perished at Vilna or Verdun; boys who sought escape from hungry villages; hobos in the making, delinquents on the make – they poured by the thousand, by the day, into Hanover. Only to find it as stricken as elsewhere. Queues – queues for everything. Cigarettes, chocolate, clothing, milk, fish, bread. No jobs which they could do, no lodgings which they could afford. Most did not want to leave again; the big city at least promised opportunities – and besides, where could they go? So they tended to congregate, a constantly increasing, floating multitude, at their point of arrival. Hanover's head railway station. There they could find shelter, company, and warmth. There they created for themselves a substitute home.

In this transformed Hanover, Haarmann fell on his feet. He made a basic living in the black market as a meat hawker; his effeminate mannerisms and falsetto voice gained him contemptuous popularity – like that of a female impersonator or an epicene droll. He augmented his income – and dressed in a little brief authority – as a paid police spy (*Anglice*, copper's nark), appointed despite, or because of, his police record (which included indecent assaults as well as burglary and fraud). He obtained relaxing entertainment at the railway station; drawn thither like the pimps to King's Cross and St Lazare. At night, he would move among the swarm of rootless boys, noting and cannily appraising each newcomer; readily invoking his official contacts if anyone challenged his role of benefactor; joyfully escorting acquiescent choices to the perilous intimacy of his basement room. Only the lucky ones escaped as walking casualties.

LEFT: Fritz Haarmann

Haarmann might have gone on undisturbed, indefinitely, had he confined his transgressions to sex. Once, when a missing boy was tracked right to his door, parental insistence compelled the police to search their colleague's hideout – and, catching him *in flagrante delicto*, reluctantly to arrest him (he was sentenced to nine months). But the German police, in general, did not harry sexual perverts, even when they were debauching juveniles. Nor did the German courts, in general, itch to punish them. The situation may have been like that held to exist at one time on the Oxford circuit, where, it was said, no jury would ever convict of buggery, 'because eleven of them don't know what it is and the twelfth does it himself'.

Haarmann could never have been dismissed as an innocuous deviant. Sex criminal of course he was – but was he a sex murderer? Were his killings part and parcel of his sexual impulses? Or were they incidental and distinct – and secondary?

In trying to answer that one must remember there were two Haarmanns. Two characters within that thick, fat frame, behind that coarse moon face. The pedlar, out for profit. The pederast, out for pleasure. That he defiled his pick-ups cannot be doubted. That he killed many, and took their belongings, cannot be doubted either. But which project was uppermost in his mind as he prowled the railway station? Which was the primary driving force – material greed or sex?

According to Haarmann, he killed in paroxysms of erotic frenzy. Criminals are not the most trustworthy guide to their own motives, but psychological probabilities support him. One cannot imagine a shrewd, experienced rogue embarking on such a systematic course of murder merely to get hold of such pitifully small possessions. Cheap cuff links. A few loose coins. A pocket comb. All such things were to be found only on the better off. Most of these boys had nothing more than the garments they stood up in. But Haarmann, particularly at a time of shortages, could not bring himself to forego such tiny trifles which chance, or his own wickedness, delivered to his hand. Besides, there was someone else who had a say. His regular partner – sexual, domestic, and professional. An elegant young man less than half his age.

Hans Grans was a homosexual queen who, in most respects, ruled his older consort. He did not object to – often encouraged – Haarmann's infidelities; he liked the implicit licence to pursue his own. He demanded a cut, though, of any residual booty, and – if his eye was taken by a suit or by a trinket – he might suggest and urge that booty should be snatched. He did not drive Haarmann to murder; Haarmann did not need driving – he murdered in hot blood. But Grans sometimes gave a prod or incentive to cold robbery, as an influential and like-minded spouse. Partners to a marriage, they shared and shared alike, for better or for worse – with one solitary exception. There is much to indicate that Grans was an accomplice, even a principal, in sodomy and murder. There is nothing to indicate that he was a principal, even an accomplice, in consuming or marketing human flesh.

Haarmann was a rarity among mass murderers, best remembered and most detested for actions other than those of which he was accused. Anthropophagy may not be among penal offences, but it offends – both morally and aesthetically – more than the gravest crime expressly recognized by law. The idea of murder does not excite such abhorrence, such revulsion, as the idea of man feeding upon man. This feeling is so universal that in civilized communities cannibalism, unlike murder, is virtually unknown. Except in mortal extremities of hunger – and very seldom even then. One human being would generally rather die than devour another. Haarmann, though, seems to have been free from this inhibition, which operates as strongly on sinners as on saints, on murderers as on missionaries. The first hint transpired in his capacity as a purveyor; supplies of smuggled meat were continually dwindling, and, as easily as he took clothes for Hans, he took the disposable parts of the carcasses for his stall. His customers, long subsisting on tainted beef or pork, accepted the peculiar flavour – and survived. It was a small step then to sampling his own wares. Impelled first, perhaps, by curiosity. Tempted to continue, one would guess, by the free meal. In the end, addicted – who knows? – to the taste.

When youths and boys from many districts were reported missing, the Hanover police displayed no excess of zeal; flotsam and jetsam, drifters, might turn up anywhere. When the remains of their remains did turn up – in the river, the police did not exhaust themselves by close investigations; fleshless skulls, whitened bones, might be anybody's. And anyway, why should they suspect 'Detective' Haarmann? But under pressure of suspicion, they carefully searched his room. Under pressure of discoveries they made there – items of property, extensive stains of blood – Haarmann admitted committing twenty-four separate murders. (As he didn't plead insanity like Christie or Haigh, that may be considered a moderate computation.) He implicated Grans – a bitchy pay-off to a lover's quarrel.

Properly, the trial should have taken place in solemn silence, interrupted only by *frissons* of sheer horror. Instead, it descended into *opéra bouffe*. Haarmann chatted to the judges, rebuked or commended witnesses, exhorted Grans – glacial beside him – to follow his honourable example and confess. He incessantly cracked 'in' jokes for the delectation of brethren and partisans in the public gallery. The music of their laughter – gratifying to his queer ego – must have been one compensation for his expected sentence.

Another – gratifying his queer spitefulness – must have been the long jail term imposed on his beloved Hans.

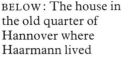

BELOW: The house in the old quarter of Hannover where Haarmann lived

Old Gaston Dominici was a peeping Tom. Not dedicated and obsessed like Byrne. But an occasional, almost accidental one. That at least is the inference I draw from the triple murder of the Drummonds in Upper Provence on 5 August 1952.

The question originally posed by this miniature massacre was: who did it? That question, though, has long since been decided. Gaston did. As a jury found proved after a twelve-day trial. The question still unanswered in many minds is: Why? What accursed combination of intent and circumstances led to an illiterate but hitherto harmless rustic slaughtering – at the age of seventy-six – three people who were strangers to him? People whom he had never before seen, whose names he did not know.

I think that, too, may now be explained with confidence. Having the advantage of time for thought and distance for perspective, one may venture to reconstruct the crimes from inception to completion.

Sir Jack Drummond was an English biochemist of international standing. During the Second World War he

BELOW: Sir Jack and Lady Drummond with ten-year-old Elizabeth

played a major part in controlling the nation's diet as Lord Woolton's right hand man at the Ministry of Food. Afterwards he was director of scientific research at Boots. In the early fifties, overwork and exhaustion laid him low. Recovering, he set off in his station wagon for a recuperative holiday abroad. With him went his wife and their ten-year-old daughter Elizabeth. They drove south across France to Villefranche on the Côte d'Azur, camping *en route* and on excursions inland. The place they picked to camp about midnight on 4 August was a hundred yards from Gaston Dominici's farm. Nearly all the Dominici family lived at or near the farm: sons, daughters, daughters-in-law, sons-in-law, grandchildren of Gaston and his wife (a toothless, withered faggot nicknamed 'the Sardine'). They were landowning peasants, comfortable financially – like the kulaks, rather than the moujiks of czarist Russia – but quintessential peasants all the same. Depending on, and obeying, the paterfamilias.

BELOW: The Dominici farm, near Forcalquier

As the head of a suburban family nightly 'locks up' his house, so old Gaston Dominici nightly 'locked up' his farm. With a gun slung on his shoulder – more from habit than for use – he patrolled the borders, alert for trespassers or poachers. Notionally a duty, this also was a pleasure. The sole chance to behave as he felt inclined. He need not do anything strenuous or useful. He could do as the poet advises – stand and stare. At the mulberry tree which he had pruned that morning. At the unforthcoming soil which he had tilled that afternoon. At the suddenly illuminated landscape as head-lamps hurried by towards Grenoble or Marseilles. Old Gaston enjoyed these solitary perambulations. Going along at a countryman's unfatiguing saunter, he would often stay out for an hour or even two. Always something to interest one who kept his eyes open.

That August night brought something exceptionally in-teresting, and the eyes of old Gaston opened wide. Some sort of a vehicle – too long for a car, too much window for a van – lay in a woody recess just off the main road. People, several people, moving to and fro; it was fine and not pitch dark, Gaston could see them clearly. Who were they? What did they want? Rather suspicious, very curious, Gaston stood and stared.

There were three of them. A man – one certainly was a man. And a woman – yes, another certainly was a woman; old Gaston appreciatively traced the rounded curves. And the third, skipping and jumping, was a child, a little girl. They were taking things from the vehicle and putting them on the ground. Sheets? Mattresses? A folding bed? Reminded old Gaston of his army bivouacking on summer manoeuvres nearly fifty years ago. His gaze firmly fixed on the gratuitous spectacle, he never moved an inch, he never made a sound.

Their preparations finished, they started to undress. Un-der the stars, in such an isolated spot, they might reasonably think themselves secure from observation. The woman, though, instinctively withdrew behind the wagon. Ironically, this took her closer to old Gaston. As the female wear was cast aside, concupiscence – long impotent or dormant – stirred his loins. Forgetful of prudence, he stepped forth to get a better view.

He was spotted instantly. They jumped to conclusions, only partly justified. If a woman, however innocently, disrobes where men may see her, she must be ready for male stares. But Lady Drummond's innate modesty was shocked; Sir Jack's nerves, after illness, were hypersensitive. He construed it as a calculated insult to his wife. Gaston may not have understood the foreign words. He fully understood the foreigner's attitude. Was he to be reviled and threatened, almost in his own domain, by an alien unauthorized intruder? Gaston's indignation boiled up and overflowed. In rage and fright, he raised his gun, levelled it . . . and, hardly realizing what he did, he fired. And, without pausing, fired again. Sir Jack fell dead.

BELOW: Gaston Dominici in court, November 1954

204

ABOVE: Dominici's family; his wife, 'the Sardine', is on the extreme right.

LEFT: The verdict is announced. Dominici was sentenced to life imprisonment

The rest was not, as superficially appears, the result of a savage running mindlessly amock. It was rather the result of reasserted peasant cunning. Murder had been done. Murder meant the guillotine. No one must live to tell the tale. And so Lady Drummond died – three bullets through her heart. And so Elizabeth, running desperately for life, was killed with the butt of a rifle in which no bullets remained.

When the police visited the Dominicis – after the bodies had been discovered by a wayfarer – nobody of course could tell them anything. 'Me? I was in bed all night,' old Gaston said, and the other members of the family rallied round. But some of them at least knew more than they at first would say, and later on at least some of these said some of it. Enough to put old Gaston behind bars, where he confessed and then retracted, time and time again, until the day he stepped into the dock. The death sentence was commuted into life imprisonment, and in 1960 he was set free on compassionate grounds. Old age.

Voyeurism – much associated with the old – is one of the milder sexual aberrations. It is not a crime, though it may give rise to one, or merge with one – most commonly, a trivial 'breach of the peace'. Here, diluted voyeurism gave rise to murder. None would have died on the Marseilles–Grenoble road that night if Sir Jack Drummond had been undressing alone.

OPPOSITE: Dominici at the age of eighty-six, shortly after his release from prison

207

CRIME WITHOUT A CRIMINAL:

CASES UNSOLVED

**Jack the Ripper
Mrs Luard**

PAGE 208: A contemporary impression of Jack the Ripper

RIGHT: *Police News*, 22nd September 1888

Under this heading, as under the heading 'Crime Without Responsibility', each case will be one of murder, but for an entirely different reason. I propose to recall two classic mysteries of crime, cases in which nobody was ever put on trial, but about which speculation is periodically renewed. And only a murder can long remain unsolved, and yet retain such a hold on public interest.

We are here confronted with inverted whodunits; all the clues – and a non-solution – handed us at the start. The ground well-trodden and intensively researched. I do not suggest that we attempt to strike out on fresh tracks. Merely retrace the steps of earlier explorers until they arrived in blind alleys, at dead ends.

Front runner as a subject for such an exercise is the series of crimes filed under the name of Jack the Ripper.

Half a dozen (maybe one more, maybe one less) common prostitutes slaughtered, apparently without motive, in the dark dens and narrow lanes of Whitechapel during the autumn months of 1888. Prostitutes of the lowest and most pitiable sort; derelict and ghastly parodies of woman-hood; drifting through a half-world of gin palaces and doss houses, selling 'short times' for a few pence to any buyer. Slaughtered with accompanying mutilations so appalling as to make Patrick Byrne appear almost wholesome. All the work, it has been generally accepted, of one individual endowed with infinite cunning, audacity – and luck.

This resumé is a reminder, not a revelation. *Everyone* knows *what* the Ripper *did*. *No one* knows, however, who the Ripper *was*. No policeman, no civilian, consciously observed him. No clue of real value or practical use was found. The Ripper's elusiveness, baulking enquiries on the spot, has continued for nearly ninety years to baulk enquirers.

The latter, both professional and amateur, are legion. Cool logicians and rabid romancers jostle one another with their fantasies and theories. Because the mutilations were supposed to indicate anatomical knowledge, if not surgical skill, the first popular inference was that the Ripper must be a doctor – an inference that has never entirely lost support and has, by natural progression, been extended to medical students, mortuary attendants, midwives (favourite among the few proponents of a female Ripper), and even – on a lower

POLICE THE ILLUSTRATED NEWS

LAW COURTS AND WEEKLY RECORD

No. 1,284.   SATURDAY, SEPTEMBER 22, 1888.   Price One Penny.

"IS HE THE WHITECHAPEL MURDERER?"

READY FOR THE WHITECHAPEL FIEND. WOMEN SECRETLY ARMED.

LATEST DETAILS OF THE WHITECHAPEL MURDERS

ANNIE CHAPMAN BEFORE AND AFTER DEATH

THE FIFTH VICTIM OF THE WHITECHAPEL FIEND.

FINDING THE MUTILATED BODY IN MITRE SQARE.

social scale – a butcher. Other specific 'suspects' include the Duke of Clarence (elder son of Edward VII, brother of George V); Sir William Gull (Physician in Ordinary to Queen Victoria); J.K. Stephen (literateur, son of 'the mad judge' who mistried Mrs Maybrick); one Druitt (an obscure young barrister); and an assortment of foreigners, seafarers – and policemen. Also nominated for the pseudonymous vacancy are two murderers already famous in their own right: Severin Klosowski, alias George Chapman, former medical orderly in the Russian army, the barber poisoner of the Borough, executed in 1903, who is known to have lived in Whitechapel during the Ripper murders; and Dr Neill Cream, poisoner of Lambeth whores, said by the hangman to have exclaimed 'I am Jack the—' as he plunged into the drop in 1892. (That Cream lay confined throughout the Ripper murders within the walls of an American penitentiary reflects on the truthfulness, not of the hangman, but of Cream.)

I shall not seek to assess the weight of these hypotheses, nor to submit an alternative of my own. I confess myself totally – and pleasurably baffled. If murder is indeed a fine art, as De Quincey (only half, I think, in jest) averred, then the Ripper is the Raphael of murderers.

OPPOSITE: Vigilante groups patrolled the East End in search of Jack the Ripper, 1888

ABOVE: Just two of the many suspects: the Duke of Clarence (left) and Sir William Gull (right)

To move from the Ripper to the Luards is to move from the gutter to society. Not the high society of the metropolitan gossip columns, but to the good society of the county and the land. Mystery, though, pays no regard to class distinctions.

In the garden of their pleasant country home in Kent, General Luard and his wife were discussing their programme for that summer afternoon.

'I think, Maggie, I'll fetch my golf bag from the clubhouse. I'll need it this weekend when we go away.'

The Luards did not have a car. In 1909 few had.

'I'll walk with you part of the way.'

The General readily agreed. Now a trim sixty-nine, he had always had an affectionate relationship with his attractive wife who, at fifty-eight, could have passed for forty-five.

'How far will you come, dear?'

'I'll turn off at the Casa.' An unoccupied bungalow in the neighbouring woods, with a fine view from the veranda. The Luards often walked there, separately or together. 'Then I can get home before Mrs Stewart arrives for tea.'

'Fine. Fine.'

They set off arm in arm. At half past two.

Actually the General arrived home first. At half past four. With his golf bag. Mrs Stewart was waiting. The General entertained her to tea, apologizing for, and expressing surprise at, Mrs Luard's absence; escorting her homewards later some way through the woods. When they parted, she saw him take the path towards the Casa. At 5.15.

At 5.30 a person living near the Casa heard shouts and ran out to come upon the General. His face distorted, his behaviour like one demented.

'Dead. Shot. Dead. Shot,' he kept repeating. He led a little group of people to the Casa.

Mrs Luard was lying face downwards. Her arms were stretched upwards, with palms outwards. Two bullets had been fired at close range through her head. Her left hand glove had been pulled off and four rings roughly taken, tearing away the skin. Her purse was missing. She had been dead, the doctors said, between two and three hours. That tied in with shots heard near the Casa at 3.15, and, not unnaturally, attributed to someone shooting rabbits.

Murder and robbery. But murder to rob, or robbery to cover murder?

At the inquest, on the first day the General told his story. Corroborated by independent witnesses. At 3.20, five minutes after the shots were heard, he was seen some fifteen minutes walk from the Casa, heading in the direction of the golf club. At 3.25 he was seen five minutes nearer the club, with the Casa correspondingly five minutes further away. At 3.30 he was seen in the club itself, 'quite as usual, not in any degree discomposed'.

That indisputable schedule was obviously significant. Not that initially any suspicion had fallen on the General. There were not the slightest grounds for it. Newspaper readers all over Britain shared his suffering.

But the coroner adjourned for a fortnight ('so that the police may continue their enquiries'), and when he sat again public feeling had undergone an unaccountable change. A vague and dreadful myth took shape; the General did it, he killed her, it was all carefully planned. Anonymous letters of execration reached the stricken widower, and at the resumed hearing, he appeared to many in the role of the accused.

Now a prey to persecution as well as grief, the General took his own life by throwing himself beneath a train. He left behind a letter to an intimate friend: 'I care for nothing except to join her again.'

The murder of Mrs Luard, after all these years, remains unsolved. One does not know who did it. But one does know who did not.

Postscript

I had meant to end with a brief statement designated 'Moral'. Remembering from the nursery that each of Aesop's fables ended with a Moral – a Stitch in Time Saves Nine, Waste Not Want Not, More Haste Less Speed, and similar precepts of equally solid worth. But these are not fables. And I am no Aesop. Besides, I have come to doubt whether any general *moral* can be extracted from the story of crime. Only some not very encouraging *conclusions* which form the stuff of what might be called my own personal credo.

I believe that, as there is pure Good in this world, there is pure Evil. Evil which takes human shape in the most heinous criminals. Evil which works through the most heinous crimes. Evil irrespective of environment or breed, which may accentuate without initiating.

I believe that pure Evil is incurable and therefore that its human vessels are irreclaimable. Which does not mean that they should be exempt from punishment, or that they are entitled to irrational indulgence. Otherwise, in practice, we equate Evil with Good.

I believe that a close study of crime and criminals – essentially changeless in a changing world – serves to promote an ethos, an attitude of mind, which can best contain, though it can never quite suppress, them. In other words, whether you have enjoyed the tour or not, it has done you no harm to have followed me so far.

Bibliography

Allen, F. L. *Only Yesterday*. New York and Harmondsworth: Harper and Row (1957) and Pelican Books (1938).

Birkenhead, First Earl of. *Famous Trials*. London: Hutchinson, 1900.

Bolitho, William. *Murder for Profit*. London: Jonathan Cape, 1926.

Borrel, Clive and Cashinella, Brian. *Crime in Britain Today*. London: Routledge & Kegan Paul, 1975.

Charnwood, Lord. *Abraham Lincoln*. London: Constable, 1916.

Cooke, Alistaire. *America*. New York and London: Knopf and BBC, 1973.

De Quincey, Thomas. *On Murder as a Fine Art*. London: Philip Allan, 1925.

Fay, E. S. *The Life of Mr. Justice Swift*. London: Methuen, 1939.

Fordham, Edward Wilfred. *Notable Cross Examinations*. Westport and London, Greenwood Press, Inc. and Constable, 1951.

Gallo, Max. *Mussolini's Italy: Twenty Years of the Facist Era*. Translated by Charles L. Markham. New York and Aylesbury: Macmillan and Abelard-Schumann, 1973.

Gillen, Mollie. *Assassination of the Prime Minister: The Shocking Death of Spencer Perceval*. New York and London: St. Martin's Press, Inc. (1973) and Sidgwick & Jackson (1972).

Giono, Jean. *The Dominici Affair*. London: Museum Press, 1956.

Hastings, Patrick. *Cases in Court*. London: Heinemann, 1949.

Hodge, J. H., ed. *Notable British Trials*. London: Hodge, 1905–59.

Hyde, H. Montgomery. *Sir Patrick Hastings: His Life and Cases*. London: Heinemann, 1960.

——— *Norman Birkett*. London: Hamish Hamilton, 1964.

Hyman, Alan. *The Rise and Fall of Horatio Bottomley*. London: Cassel, 1972.

Kefauver, Estes. *Crime in America*. Edited by Sidney Shallett. Westport and London: Greenwood Press, Inc. (1968) and Victor Gollancz (1951).

Kenny, C. S. and Turner, J. *Outlines of Criminal Law*. Cambridge: Cambridge University Press, 1902–72.

Kobler, John. *Capone*. New York and London: Fawcett World (1975) and Coronet Books (1973).

Lustgarten, Edgar. *A Century of Murderers*. London: Eyre Methuen, 1976.

Mackenzie, F. A. *The Thaw Case*. London: Geoffrey Bles, 1928.

Majoribanks, Edward. *The Life of Sir Edward Marshall Hall*. London: Victor Gollancz, 1929.

Maxwell, Ronald. *The Jersey Monster*. London: W. H. Allen, 1972.

McKernan, Maureen. *The Amazing Crime and Trial of Leopold and Loeb*. London: Signet Books, 1957.

Minney, R. J. *Rasputin*. New York and London: David McKay, Co. Inc. (1973) and Cassel (1972).

Odell, Robin. *Jack the Ripper in Fact and Fiction*. London: Harrap, 1965.

Parry, Edward. *The Drama of the Law*. Tonbridge: Ernest Benn, 1924.

Pearson, John. *The Profession of Violence*. London: Weidenfeld & Nicolson, 1972.

Rae, George W., ed. *Confessions of the Boston Strangler*. London: Tandem-Ortolan, 1967.

Salvemini, Gaetano. *The Origins of Fascism in Italy*. Translated by Roberto Vivarelli. New York and London: Harper and Row (1972, 1973).

Samuels, Charles. *The Girl in the Red Velvet Swing*. New York: Gold Medal Books, n.d.

Sorenson, Theodore C. *Kennedy*. New York and London: Harper and Row and Hodder & Stoughton, 1965.

Still, Larry. *The Limits of Sanity*. Toronto: McClelland & Stewart, 1972.

Traini, Robert. *Murder for Sex*. London: William Kimber, 1960.

Walker-Smith, Derek. *Lord Reading and his Cases*. London: Chapman & Hall, 1934.

Webb, Duncan. *Crime is my Business*. London: Frederick Muller, 1953.

Whitcomb, J. F. *Trial of Alfredo Messina*. Amsterdam: W.L.A. Publications, n.d.

Wilson, Colin and Pitman, Patricia. *Encyclopedia of Murder*. London: Arthur Barker, 1961.

Acknowledgments

Pages 2–3, left to right (top) Popperfoto, Radio Times Hulton Picture Library, Keystone; (bottom) Radio Times Hulton Picture Library, Popperfoto, Keystone; Pages 6–7, left, Radio Times Hulton Picture Library, Mansell Collection; Page 12, Weidenfeld and Nicolson Archives; Pages 14–15, Mitchell Library, Sydney; Page 16, Keystone; Page 17, Camera Press; Page 18, Keystone; Page 21, Popperfoto; Page 23, Popperfoto; Page 24, Radio Times Hulton Picture Library; Page 25, Camera Press; Page 26, Keystone; Page 27, Keystone; Page 28, Camera Press; Page 30, Press Association; Page 33, the *People*; Page 35, top, Keystone, bottom, John Frost, World Wide Newspaper Collector's Club; Page 36, top, Popperfoto, bottom, *Sunday Times*; Page 39, *Daily Express*/by Terry Disney; Page 41, London Express Pictures; Page 42, John Frost, World Wide Newspaper Collector's Club; Page 46, London Express Pictures; Page 47, Radio Times Hulton Picture Library; Page 51, Central Press Photos Ltd; Page 52, Popperfoto; Page 54, Radio Times Hulton Picture Library; Page 55, *Daily Mirror*; Page 58, Radio Times Hulton Picture Library; Page 61, Central Press Photos Ltd; Page 62, Popperfoto; Page 64, Radio Times Hulton Picture Library; Page 65, Fox Photos; Page 68, Radio Times Hulton Picture Library; Page 72, National Portrait Gallery, Washington, Smithsonian Institute; Page 73, Library of Congress/Orbis Publishing; Page 75, John Frost, World Wide Newspaper Collector's Club; Page 76, Library of Congress/Orbis Publishing; Page 78, John Frost, World Wide Newspaper Collector's Club; Page 80, Mansell Collection; Page 81, By gracious permission of HM The Queen; Page 83, Radio Times Hulton Picture Library; Page 86, Press Association; Page 87, Press Association; Page 89, top, Associated Press; bottom, Popperfoto; Page 92, Lincoln National Life Foundation, Fort Wayne, Indiana; Page 94, left, Lincoln National Life Foundation, right, Radio Times Hulton Picture Library; Page 95, Popperfoto; Page 96, Library of Congress; Page 98, Popperfoto; Page 100, John Frost, World Wide Newspaper Collector's Club; Page 103, Foto Italia; Page 105, Keystone; Page 106, Keystone; Page 107, Fox Photos; Page 108, Mondadori; Page 109, Becco Giallo/Coll Moro, Milan; Page 110, Popperfoto; Page 112, Keystone; Page 113, top, Associated Press; bottom, Keystone; Page 115, Mansell Collection; Page 116, Keystone; Page 118, Radio Times Hulton Picture Library; Page 121, Keystone; Page 122, Keystone; Page 123, Keystone; Page 124, Wide World Photos; Page 126, Keystone; Page 127, Associated Press; Page 128, Canadian Press Picture Service; Page 131, Keystone; Page 132, Keystone; Page 133, Keystone; Page 134, Keystone; Page 135, Keystone; Page 138, Popperfoto; Page 139, top, Popperfoto; bottom, Keystone; Page 140, Popperfoto; Page 142, Popperfoto; Page 145, Press Association; Page 148, John Frost, World Wide Newspaper Collector's Club; Page 151, John Frost, World Wide Newspaper Collector's

Index

gangsters shoot twice in Fulham street

LONDON BID TO KILL KRAY CASE WITNESS

John Gialdini, who said Hatry's counsel suggested the duplication of stock.

ARREST THESE FOUR MEN

ey are the mpire in th

ay 'The People' has fo the facts about a vice the heart of London a national scandal.

MYSTERY OF THE DEATH OF THE MONK RASPUTIN.

By JOHN STEVENS

ASTS from a shotgun were Ir. Charles Mitchell, a key on witness in the Kray three years ago, outside am home today. He was

ll, aged 42 and 6ft. 3in tall was his own car, parked outside his Clehre Street, Fulham, when the ned fir

old detectives he noticed a 1964 blue at the other side of the road. There was the wheel, and another in the back seat to open the door of the car, say the at seat of the Cortina levelled a revolver at it him.

ts house

ducked and the blast passed over his ailed the window of his next-door neigh ber two children w here Mrs Sue D ahed ran for cove red their sh and raced away who was seen by ay to have a

Mr Mitchell al the Bow Work of A and Wadsworth a boad and be was a second

At Great ather funny well a about had passed street every M. Peter the shooting hold

or car SEC running r Cot he to Boyd The ure has happens M

r Cat for L in the

Sex case sensation

COURT SEES THIS MASK AND COAT OF NAILS

PRESI IS KI

Texas Snipe Johnson

LAVEMASTER' ATTILIO MESSIN
TS FOUR YEARS

By TONY CONYERS

VICE king Attilio Messina, 48, who "enslaved" a woman for ten years, was gaoled at the Old Bailey yesterday for four years.
The woman he was said to have enslaved is Mrs. Edna Kallman, 39. The court was told that she worked as a Mayfair prostitute for Messina, and that
● She earned £60,000 in the ten years and handed it all to Messina.
● She was allowed £7 a week to pay for her hairdresser, telephone and food.
● She was forced by violence and threats to "work" every day of the week, whether she was well or ill.
Messina, otherwise known as Raymond Maynard, pleaded guilty to procuring Mrs. Kallman to be come a common prostitute and to bring on the earnings of prosti

—Then he will have to

"You apparently for ten years have made a sumptuous revolting type of living from the suffering bodies of wom you trapped, seduced and reduced to a form of slavery... have caused great suffering and it is only right and just th you also should suffer"
—The judge, SIR GERALD DODSON, sentencing Messina yes

THE FIVE EVIL BROTHERS
REIGNED BY TE

By TOM TULLETT
Chief of the Mirror Crime Bureau
THE five evil Messina brothers, vice kings in London for more than twenty years, are finally smashed.
They brought organised vice to London to a main known before only in Chicago.
And they used Chicago methods of torts and fear

They ran a vice